How to prevent breast cancer
or stop it returning

New evidence reveals
amazing protector foods

HILDA GLICKMAN

BSc (Hons), MA, BPhil, DipION, Cert Health Prom

W. Foulsham & Co. Ltd
For Foulsham Publishing Ltd

The Old Barrel Store, Brewery Courtyard, Draymans Lane, Marlow, Bucks, SL7 2FF

Foulsham books can be found in all good bookshops and direct from www.foulsham.com

ISBN: 978-0-572-04543-2

Copyright © 2015 Hilda Glickman

A CIP record for this book is available from the British Library

The moral right of the author has been asserted

Disclaimer
This book is intended for information purposes only. It is not intended to be a substitute for medical treatment or advice. If you suspect that you have a medical problem, it is important that you see a qualified medical practitioner. If you are undergoing medical treatment for any condition, consult your physician for advice before taking any supplements or changing your diet.

Typeset in Great Britain by Chris Brewer Origination
Printed and bound in Great Britain by Martins the Printers Ltd

This book is dedicated to my parents,
Malkie and Sam Harris

'I accepted with enthusiasm the opportunity to review this excellent book. This is clearly well written and well researched. I would agree with the explanation and advice for the different lifestyle and additional strategies, which the book comprehensively reviews.

It is also written in a pleasant and approachable style, which makes the information, of which there is a great deal, easier to absorb.

I would highly recommend it to anyone considering conducting a nutritional lifestyle change after cancer, or those who are considering changing their lifestyle to prevent cancer.'

Robert Thomas MRCP MD FRCR
Professor of Post Graduate Medicine Cranfield University
Consultant Oncologist Bedford and Addenbrooke's Hospitals

Contents

Acknowledgements

I very much want to thank the following people for all the help and advice they have given me during the writing of this book:

Janice Grant, Ann Spencer, Linda and Joe Caplin, Minna Harris, Laurie Bernard, my children Shona and Paul, and especially Richard, who has commented helpfully and extensively on the content of the book.

An extra very special thanks goes to my husband Avrom who has helped, supported and encouraged me all through this project and with everything else that I do.

Introduction

It might take you ten minutes to read the first few chapters of this book. In that time, another woman in the UK will be diagnosed with breast cancer. The numbers are getting higher and this is not just because we are living longer. The fact is that women are succumbing to the disease at ever-younger ages. Getting a diagnosis can be shattering. Although thankfully many women survive breast cancer, the research suggests there are things we can do to prevent getting it in the first place.

In the UK, one woman in eight will get the disease at some time in her life. The thought of breast cancer strikes fear in many of us. Those who have seen relatives succumb to it often fear a genetic link. However, most cancers are not genetically related. For breast cancer, it is only about five per cent.

Why do we need to think about cancer? Well, the latest research suggests that we can have microscopic tumours in our bodies that never develop into anything serious. Many people have these but they are kept in check by their immune systems. We make cancerous cells all the time but our body usually deals with them. This book is about strengthening your immune system. A vast amount of new research shows that this can be possible.

This book gives you all the very latest information to help you make your body as healthy as possible and to protect you from breast cancer. The good news is that cancer does not manifest overnight. It takes many years to develop and goes through various stages. These are initiation, promotion, progression, actual cancer and spread of cancer. This means that before a cancer is actually there we often have time to do something before microscopic cells develop into full-blown cancer. In the following pages you will see that what we eat and what we do can have a powerful effect on disease prevention and on our health in general.

The aim of this book

The aim of this book is to bring to the attention of women everywhere all the research that has been carried out in recent years, showing the amazing power of ordinary foods to protect us and save us from developing this frightening disease. It is for those who want to prevent getting the disease in the first place and for those who have had breast cancer and want to help stop it returning. It is not, however, about treating actual cancer and is not a substitute for medical treatment.

There is so much evidence that breast cancer can be prevented nutritionally that it is overwhelming. Yet even though this evidence has been published in scientific and medical journals, most of it is still sitting gathering dust in the British Library and other places. Because of this, the main aim of the book is to bring to you this amazing information so that you can protect yourself from nature's onslaughts. Prevention really is better than cure and I believe that we should do all we can to protect ourselves. This is empowering and can be interesting and enjoyable at the same time.

More and more, health practitioners are coming round to the idea that what we do in our own lives can affect our health. This has certainly been the case with regard to heart disease, where healthy eating and taking exercise have been highly promoted. It used to be thought that breast cancer was different but now we know that this too is affected by what we do and what we eat. By taking steps to improve our health overall we can make our bodies less hospitable to cancer.

If you have had breast cancer, what now?

Your treatment is over. Do you feel relieved or is there a sense of insecurity? Do you feel that you are now alone and are not sure how to proceed? Do you wonder if you should eat differently or just go on as before?

After treatment, some people just want to forget the whole thing and go back to life as they lived it before. Others get depressed even though their tumour has gone because suddenly they are out on their own. They feel lost and are not sure what to do next.

The problem is that the illness is not just the tumour. Medical treatment can get rid of the tumour and other cancerous cells around the body. However, the underlying condition of the body that allowed the tumour to grow in the first place may not have changed. But you can change it.

Become more resistant

You can make your body more or less hospitable to cancer. For example, if you have too much chronic inflammation, too much insulin or poor immunity you are not giving yourself the best chance of staying healthy. This book can show you how to make your body as resistant to breast cancer as it can be.

When talking about bacteria, Louis Pasteur said that the germ is nothing, the terrain is everything. By 'terrain' Pasteur meant the underlying condition of the body. We see this all the time when infectious diseases are going around: some succumb to it while others don't. This is because some people have stronger immune systems than others. Cancer, of course, is not an infectious disease but the underlying condition of the body is still important. This is what is meant by the 'terrain'. We can make the body more resistant by what we eat and what we do. We do have the ability to change our terrain.

Put yourself in control

So much information on breast cancer prevention now exists so why not make use of it? It is not difficult because it involves ordinary, delicious foods that you can prepare quickly and easily. These are not strange or odd items but the foods that have sustained us for thousands of years.

Learning all you can about the latest research on breast cancer and nutrition can be exciting, empowering and satisfying. New studies are being published all the time. Many people have changed their diets and done very well as a result. You can too.

However, food is not the only thing that can help us. Other factors like stress, poor sleep and chemicals in the environment can also affect our chances of getting cancer. This book will also show you how to reduce stress, make your environment safer and get a good night's sleep.

What you do will not be a guarantee of success, however. It is all about reducing the risk. We take care when we cross the road in order to reduce our risk of being knocked down. We know that this is not a guarantee but we try to do our best anyway. This is what following the guidance in this book can do for you. It can help reduce your risk.

CHAPTER 1

Preventing breast cancer with foods

In the chapters that follow, you will find many ways to make our bodies less susceptible to breast cancer by making them as healthy as possible. Some of these are related to the amazing anti-cancer properties in fruit and vegetables.

The power of phytochemicals

Every year more and more studies are carried out which show how common foods can help prevent us succumbing to cancer. In the past, nutritionists and scientists thought that foods just contained vitamins, minerals, protein, fats and carbohydrates. Very recently, however, discoveries have been made that certain foods contain thousands of other substances that can help prevent cancer in many ways. These are mostly found in plant foods such as fruit, vegetables, nuts and seeds and a few animal foods such as fish.

In the last twenty years or so, scientists have discovered a wealth of cancer-preventive chemicals in ordinary plant foods. They are called phytochemicals, from the Greek word 'phyto', meaning plant. In this book, you will see which foods hold these secrets and how they work.

Phytochemicals exist to protect plants from pollution, predators and weather. As they are rooted to the ground, plants cannot move to protect themselves, as can animals, so they produce these chemicals instead. They are not nutrients because we do not need them to live, but they are extremely protective to us in so many ways.

The rich, brilliant colours of fruit and vegetables and their particular smells are due to these phytochemicals. For example, carotenoids in carrots give them their vibrant orange colour, and anthocyanins in prunes and blueberries give them their blue, black and purple colours. The indoles in cabbages give them their pungent odour and allicin in garlic gives it its very distinctive taste. There are so many phytochemicals that it is overwhelming. In fact it is estimated that there are around 4,000 in various plants that can affect health, probably more. Not only that, but each food item can contain hundreds of phytochemicals itself. Garlic alone has around 200, turmeric has around 90 and these are just the ones that have been discovered. In the chapters that follow, we will look at the ones that are most important for breast cancer protection.

What can they do for us?

Phytochemicals do not just protect plants. They also protect us. Research has shown that they can do many of the things that pharmaceutical companies have been trying to do for years. For example, they can stop microscopic cancer cells in test tubes getting the blood supply they need to grow, they can make oestrogen less dangerous, they can cause microscopic cells to self-destruct and they can help detoxify toxic chemicals via the liver. This book will show you exactly what these plants can do for us, how they do it and how you can use them to your advantage.

Why 'just eat a balanced diet' is wrong

You may have read or you may have been told to 'just eat a balanced diet'. This is the same as being told to 'eat a good diet'. It is actually true by definition but means almost nothing. This is because it does not tell us what a balanced diet actually is, and more often than not people interpret this as just eating a bit of everything in the supermarket. Also, what seems to be a balanced diet to one person might be a very poor diet to another. For example, how many portions of fruit and vegetables should we eat; how much meat? Should you have some crisps in a balanced diet? Therefore, if you read that statement again, you will see that people who say this are not really telling you anything.

The following chapters will show you what the right diet contains. They go into very specific detail based on research contained in scientific and medical journals. This book is full of good news and hope, and there is ample evidence that we have the right to hope. For those who fear getting breast cancer and those who have been treated for it, this book will show you which foods can reduce your risk and how they do it.

Enjoy your cancer-protective foods

I cannot stress enough that I hope you will enjoy protecting yourself with these delicious foods. Food should be enjoyed yet, too often, it is seen as a penance, with people telling you not to eat the things you like and to eat all the things you do not like.

Likewise, preventing cancer should also be fun and interesting, not a bind and a chore. It does not need to have complicated recipes or be time-consuming. In short, it does not need to be a real burden. I hope you will find what I have to tell you in the next few chapters exciting and empowering.

We cannot change our genes, we cannot change our environment, but we can control our diet and lifestyle. Why not make this work for you?

CHAPTER 2
Who gets breast cancer?

Breast cancer is found all over the world. However, there are big differences between the numbers of sufferers in different countries. In general the more westernised and industrialised the country, the greater the incidence of breast cancer. Places like North America, Northern Europe, Australia and New Zealand have much higher rates than China, Korea and Japan. The scale of difference now seen between these countries is dramatic.

In the UK, about 88 women in 100,000 will develop breast cancer, while in Thailand only eight in 100,000 will do so. This is a huge difference. The highest rates of cancer generally are in Eastern European countries such as Hungary and the Czech Republic. Their rate is 300 to 400 cases per 100,000.

Since there is such a huge difference between these countries and the UK and USA, you might think that this is genetic. However, when people from these low incidence countries migrate to high incidence countries their cancer rate begins to mirror that of their new country. This means that something other than genetics is going on.

In addition to this, although rates in these countries are lower they are starting to creep up. This is because people in these countries are beginning to eat foods imported from the West. They are also adopting a more westernised lifestyle. For example, Japan, Singapore and Korea were once renowned for their extremely low rates but studies have shown that cases in these countries have doubled or tripled in the last 40 years.

In China, there has been a 20 to 30 per cent increase in the last decade. The cause of this is thought to be a sedentary workforce, delays in child bearing and a westernised diet including drinking more alcohol. Rates in other low and middle-income countries are also rising. You can see therefore how important diet and lifestyle is. This then is what we will look at in the chapters that follow.

An interesting fact is that, in China, breast cancer used to be called the 'rich woman's disease' because richer women succumbed to it more than poorer women. Even in Western countries, there are more instances of higher class women getting breast cancer than lower class or poorer women. This might be because they are more likely to have taken HRT. Another reason might be that they were 'better fed' as children and ate more meat so they reached puberty earlier.

What is the difference between East and West?

One of the biggest differences in food consumption between the East and the West is the huge amount of processed foods eaten in countries like the UK, the USA and Australia. In the East, women tend to eat more fruit, vegetables and fish.

However, if you look closely and study what people actually eat all over the world, you will see that they have all sorts of different diets. It is not always easy to find groups who still eat their traditional diet but they can be found. For example, the Masai eat a diet high in meat and milk, Eskimos eat whale meat, people in India eat a vegetarian diet full of peas, beans, lentils and yogurt, and they all do very well. In the Mediterranean, they traditionally eat lots of fruit, vegetables and oily fish, and this has been considered one of the healthiest diets in the world. So, if people all over the world can eat all different diets, does that mean that we should just eat anything?

The answer is, of course, no, although you often hear people making this claim. Why then do people all over the world eat different foods but many remain healthy? The fact is that we can eat different things but only do well if these foods are unprocessed. This is the crucial point. Much of the arguments about whether we should eat meat or not, whether we should eat fish or not, and so on, are related to how we are producing the food itself, how the animals are reared and fed, and the way in which the foods are processed.

Food production

One of the main problems about Western food is the way it is produced. Is your meat full of antibiotics and steroids? Have your farmed fish been fed small fish (plankton) which is their traditional food or have they been given cereals instead? Have your vegetables been organically grown or been sprayed with lots of different pesticides? One study found 11 different pesticides on one piece of lettuce.

Populations do very well on their traditional unprocessed natural diet. However, when peoples start processing their food too much, and food becomes different from what it should be, the trouble starts. Research has shown that it takes about 20 years for this to happen.

The bottom line

The bottom line on diet and health generally is that we should be consuming food that is as similar to its natural state as possible. This means natural, organically grown, fresh produce rather than foods made from these. It is better to eat a whole apple rather than apple pie or apple juice. It is better to eat fresh fish rather than tinned, smoked or salted fish. You might think that this is rather boring, but it need not be, given the vast amounts of different fruit and vegetables that are available in the modern supermarket.

We should also consume a larger variety of these foods. In times past, we were hunter-gatherers. When what we could find was used up in one area, we moved to another. This made us consume many different types of plant foods, a much wider range than we do today. In addition to this, we had to eat different foods at different times of the year because there was no refrigeration or freezing. This meant that we ingested different nutrients throughout the year. These days we can eat the same foods all year round. This is not good because it can reduce our nutrient intake.

In the following chapters, you will not only learn which foods can prevent breast cancer but also how they do it. This is based on findings from scientific and medical journals using various types of research methods. These are:

- Looking at breast cancer rates in different countries (epidemiology).

- Comparing the diets of women with breast cancer to women who are similar in other ways but who don't have the disease. Sometimes sisters are studied (case control studies).

- Asking women to record what they eat over some years and noting who gets the disease in relation to their diet. Often thousands of women are studied (prospective cohort studies).

- Studies where genetically identical mice are given different diets and the results compared (animal trials).

- Studies of cancer cells placed in glass with a food substance (in vitro studies).

CHAPTER 3
Put out the fire: reducing inflammation

I am sure you know what inflammation is and have suffered from it from time to time. When we hurt our bodies, they can become inflamed. We can see this easily on our skin. If we cut ourselves or get a bite from an insect, it becomes red, hot and painful. It can become swollen too. Inflammation is designed to help your body heal by bringing blood with its nutrients and oxygen to the site. However, if there is too much inflammation, we experience pain to no good effect. Sufferers of arthritis will tell you how painful it can be when their joints become inflamed. The 'itis' part of a diagnosis means inflammation, so tendonitis just means inflammation in the tendons, tonsillitis means inflammation in the tonsils and colitis means inflammation of the colon.

Inflammation and cancer

However, what has all this to do with cancer? The problem is that too much inflammation can increase your risk of getting all kinds of cancer, including breast cancer. The good news, on the other hand, is that if you eat anti-inflammatory foods or take natural anti-inflammatory supplements, you can reduce your chances of suffering from inflammation and getting cancer at the same time. This is because these foods can lower an important chemical called COX-2.

Chronic inflammation can make cancer cells proliferate and spread. Inflammation can also promote tumour growth and make your immune system weaker so that there is less defence against cancerous cells. It can also increase the blood supply to new tumours, which helps them grow, and allow cancer cells to move about the body by breaking down the fibrous material that surrounds them. It both causes and drives cancer.

Those with more inflammation tend to have more cancer and vice versa. Luckily, taking steps to control inflammation can go a long way to protect your body from this and other diseases.

Foods can lower the COX-2 enzyme. But what is this?

An enzyme is just a substance that speeds up a chemical change. One enzyme that you hear about repeatedly in relation to cancer is the COX-2 enzyme (cyclooxygenase-2).

This particular enzyme can be a real thorn in our flesh because it speeds up the production of chemicals that promote inflammation. The COX-2 enzyme is very important because it is involved in the initiation and growth of different kinds of cancers including breast cancer. It makes cells start dividing and growing and it stops cancer cells from dying normally.

For a tumour to grow, it needs nutrients and oxygen just like any other living thing. In order to get these, new blood vessels need to be produced to establish a blood supply. The COX-2 enzyme can encourage the growth of these blood vessels and help promote the growth of the cancer.

It has been found that women who have too much COX-2 are more likely to have their tumours return after a short time. Therefore, lowering levels of this enzyme or keeping these at a healthy level is very important. Dr Keith Block from the Block Center for Integrative Cancer Treatment in the USA argues that reducing inflammation makes your body less hospitable to cancer. Fortunately, this can be achieved by eating the right foods rather than having to take drugs.

How can we reduce inflammation naturally?

Foods such as fresh fruit, vegetables and oily fish contain hundreds of compounds that can help reduce inflammation. Included in these are a class of compounds known as flavonoids, of which there are over 5,000. They do a fantastic job by preventing cancers getting the blood supply they need to grow, making cancer cells self-destruct and acting as powerful antioxidants.

Below are some tips on how to reduce inflammation and keep this enzyme in check.

- Use turmeric. This is one of the most potent natural anti-inflammatory substances in existence. One study found that turmeric was as effective as cortisone in reducing inflammation. It works by enabling your body to produce cortisone naturally and to become more sensitive to it. Eat it with pepper and some fat.

- Drink green tea. Green tea has many anti-cancer properties, one of which is to reduce inflammation.

- Eat flavonoid-rich foods. These are not just strong antioxidants but are also anti-inflammatory. Of all fruit tested, cherries and raspberries have the highest anti-inflammatory effect, with blueberries, blackberries and strawberries close behind.

- Eat other anti-inflammatory foods such as broccoli, cucumbers, onions, parsley and sweet potatoes.

- Use spices and herbs like mint, mustard, nutmeg and oregano. Ginger is a potent anti-inflammatory that may also play a role in the prevention of Alzheimer's disease.

- Eat oily fish. Eating the right kind of fat is one of the most effective ways to reduce inflammation through diet. This has been shown to lower levels of inflammatory markers in the blood, proving that inflammation has indeed been reduced. One study found that oily fish was as effective as a popular anti-inflammatory drug in reducing the pain of arthritis. Two or three servings a week can help in this way.

- Eat less beef, milk, cheese, pork, egg yolk and poultry to reduce inflammation.

- Cut hydrogenated fats (the ones that are solid at room temperature like margarine) right out (see chapter 24). Some supermarkets have even stated in their promotional material that they do not use any hydrogenated fats in their products.

- Cut out all processed oils. These are sometimes described as having omega-6 and we do need this, but not from processed oils. This means eat no corn oil, safflower oil, sunflower oil, rapeseed oil or foods made from them. Fresh nuts and seeds will give us omega-6.

- Do not smoke and try not to breathe in other people's smoke. Luckily, smoking in restaurants and pubs has now been banned in the UK. In my opinion, this is one of the best health promotion initiatives that has come about in modern times.

- Avoid heavy drinking as this increases inflammation.

- Get enough sleep. Poor sleep can raise the body's level of inflammation.

- Keep your home and your body as toxin free as possible (see chapter 28).

Supplements

Supplements to reduce inflammation are also available. If you are a breast cancer survivor, it is important to ask your doctor if it is all right for you to take these. These might include combinations of the herb boswellia, bromelain from pineapple, ginger, turmeric and the herb holy basil. Combinations of these are available in health food shops.

Tests for inflammation

If you are concerned about your levels of inflammation, and certainly if you are a survivor of cancer, you should ask your GP to test you for C-reactive protein and ESR (erythrocyte sedimentation rate). If you have abnormal chronic inflammation you could take steps to reduce this and then have it tested again to make sure that it has gone down.

CHAPTER 4
Oxidation: the case of the brown apple

You are making an apple pie. You cut up the apples and then find you don't have enough flour. You go to the shop and get some. When you come back, the apple has turned brown. This is the effect of oxidation. The annoying rust on your car is another example. However, what have brown apples and rust got to do with breast cancer? The answer is that oxidation can affect our bodies as well as our apples and cars. If you can control this, you should go a long way in keeping yourself healthy and free from cancer, along with other problems like heart disease. Oxidation is not good but you can lower it dramatically by eating the right foods. An added bonus is that this should also help you age more slowly.

We, of course, need oxygen to live but it can also affect our bodies in a bad way and cause cancerous changes. The good thing is that many foods contain high levels of substances which can prevent this. These are called antioxidants and if you make fruit salads, you probably know all about them without realising it. A good example is vitamin C. If you leave the cut up apple in a solution of vitamin C, it will not go brown. Cooks know this and often soak their fruit in fruit juice to keep them fresh. Fruit juice is high in antioxidants. Food companies use antioxidants like vitamin C in their products to stop them going rancid. Therefore, not all food additives are bad. Some like vitamin C are fine, so when you see the words 'ascorbic acid' on a food packet, do not be concerned. It is just vitamin C.

What are free radicals?

Oxidation in humans is not exactly the same as rusting in cars but it can still be damaging to the body. Very many studies have shown that those eating foods high in antioxidants are less likely to get cancer. They work by stopping chemicals called free radicals doing damage. Free radicals are molecules that are unbalanced. They are lacking a particle called an electron. Because of this, they want to 'steal' an electron from another atom. They are like unguided missiles, which cause chaos, and ultimately damage our DNA.

They can also damage the cells that line our blood vessels. This can make it easier for cancer cells to get into your bloodstream, thereby allowing them to travel all over the body. Cancer cells themselves produce free radicals at a much higher rate than normal cells. These in turn produce more cancer growth and so on. Free radicals can actually disable genes that suppress cancer growth and activate genes that promote tumour growth.

Therefore, if we can prevent this happening we have gone a long way in preserving our health. In one study of 363 breast cancer patients, those with the highest levels of fat damaged by oxygen (free radical damage) were twice as likely to experience a recurrence of their cancer as those with the lowest levels. Another study in the scientific journal *Cancer Research* found that, 'risk was greatest among women who consumed lower amounts of dietary antioxidants and was minimal among higher consumers...'

Fight the free radicals

Free radicals come from our diet and the environment. Smoking, factory pollution, radiation from the sun and browned or burnt foods all produce free radicals and we are all exposed to them every day. This means that the more foods containing antioxidants that we can eat, the better. Antioxidants are called 'free radical scavengers' as they mop up these nasty chemicals. They also stop cancer cells changing to a more aggressive form and slow the rate at which they divide and multiply. Another wonderful thing that they do is to encourage cancer cells to die (apoptosis).

The good news is that there are many tasty and delicious foods which are very high in antioxidants that can protect us, so we can increase our antioxidant status by eating these every day. It is important to eat a variety of these as one or two foods alone will not do it.

There is ample evidence in medical literature to show that this is the case. The US Food and Drug Administration have produced a table of free radical scavenging foods. Those highest on the list are the most potent. ORAC means Oxygen Radical Absorbance Capacity. It is a measure of the antioxidant capacity of various foods. This is not an exhaustive list, there are of course many others, but these are just those with the highest antioxidant rating.

Food	ORAC values per five grams	Serving size	ORAC value per serving
Prunes	288.50	1 pitted prune	462
Raisins	141.50	¼ cup	1019
Blueberries	111.70	½ cup	1620
Garlic	96.95	1 clove	58
Kale	88.50	½ cup (cooked)	1150
Cranberries	87.50	½ cup	831
Strawberries	76.80	½ cup	831
Raspberries	61.35	½ cup	755
Spinach (raw)	60.50	1 cup	678
Plums	47.45	1 plum	626
Alfalfa sprouts	46.55	1 cup	307
Spinach (steamed)	45.45	½ cup (cooked)	1089
Broccoli florets	44.40	½ cup (cooked)	817
Beets	42.05	½ cup (cooked)	715
Avocados	39.10	½ avocado	149
Oranges	37.50	1 orange	982
Grapes (red)	36.95	10 grapes	177
Peppers (red)	36.55	1 medium	540

Cherries	33.50	10 cherries	455
Kiwi fruit	30.25	1 fruit	458
Baked Beans	25.15	½ cup	640
Grapefruit (pink)	24.15	½ fruit	580
Kidney beans	23.00	½ cup (cooked)	400
Onions	22.45	½ cup (chopped)	360
Grapes (white)	22.30	10 grapes	107
Corn	20.10	½ cup (cooked)	330
Aubergines	19.30	½ cup (cooked)	185

Some of the foods in the table are lower down than you might expect. For example, we know that broccoli is highly protective but does not rank highly here. However, preventing oxidation is not the only way that foods can fight cancer. For example, broccoli has other anti-cancer chemicals such as sulforaphane and indole-3-carbinol, which we will discuss in later chapters.

In addition, the antioxidant level may change depending on how the food is produced. Dried fruit like prunes are very high in antioxidants because the fruit is more concentrated. Prunes are just dried plums. The best idea is to eat a large variety of different fruit and vegetables, preferably organic, but try to incorporate those at the top of the list.

Eat a rainbow

Make your food world a colourful place because, as mentioned before, it is the colours and pigments of fruit and vegetables that contain the highest levels of antioxidants. Each different colour or pigment in these foods is related to different plant chemicals that can affect cancer in different ways. It is therefore a good idea to eat a large variety of them. Blue, black and purple fruit contain cancer-protecting anthocyanins, while yellow fruit and vegetables contain lutein and zeaxanthin, which are wonderful for the health of our eyes. Thousands of plant chemicals, some of which have only recently been discovered, are contained in these plants. Every day, new research is published in this area. This is very exciting because the foods are readily available, often easy and quick to prepare and many find them delicious to eat.

Beige is fine for your lounge

I remember that there used to be a programme about healthy eating on the television. The presenter would lay out a table with all the foods that a particular person had eaten throughout the week and another table with all the foods that he or she should have eaten. What struck me when glancing at the two tables was that the first was all full of beige-coloured foods – pies, chips, crisps, biscuits, buns, cakes, sausage rolls and battered fish, and the other table was filled with all the colours of the rainbow – the reds, blues, blacks, greens and oranges from all the fresh fruit and vegetables. These looked beautiful, alive, vibrant and healthy, while the other foods looked just like lumps of stodge. Therefore, generally speaking, the colour beige is fine for decorating your home but not for putting into your body. Some beige foods, of course, are fine. Foods such as millet, brown rice and quinoa are delicious and nutritious. However, these should be eaten in addition to the colourful fruit and vegetables, rather than instead of them.

Use spices and herbs

With regard to preventing oxidation, it is a great idea to include many different spices in your diet. For example, oregano has more than forty times the antioxidant capacity of apples and four times that of blueberries. Other important spices are rosemary, cloves, sage, cinnamon, cumin and paprika. The whole plants are better than the ground versions.

Eat them together

Research has shown that eating these fruit and vegetables together enhances their protective value. Eating one fruit such as blueberries is helpful and eating raspberries alone is also helpful, but eating two or three fruits together has an extra effect over and above the value of the two individual fruits. This is called synergy, where the effect of two substances (or more) together is greater than the effect of the sum of the two used separately. This means that here two plus two is not four but could be six or eight or even more.

One study found that when grapes, onions and adzuki beans were combined in pairs 'unique interactions were observed that were not seen when individual extracts were used'. When these were introduced alone they did not stop cancer cells proliferating as much as when used together. Another example is green tea, which can greatly enhance the effect of turmeric.

Some foods do not have cancer protective qualities themselves but can enhance the effect of those that do. An example of this is piperine, a substance present in pepper. According to Béliveau and Gingras, piperine enhances the absorption of curcumin by a factor of 1,000. Curcumin is found in turmeric. So make sure you add pepper to your turmeric-rich soups and stews and maybe have a cup of green tea with your meal.

Mixing foods together, therefore, is very important for cancer protection. This is why homemade smoothies, soups and stews are so valuable. In these dishes, you mix and ingest two, three or even more different sorts of phytochemicals at once. Nutritious and delicious!

How to lower free radical damage

- Eat good quantities of the foods recommended in this book. Mix some together for a more powerful effect.

- Do not smoke. Tobacco contains more than one hundred billion free radicals per puff. Stay away from passive smoke.

- Do not allow yourself to burn in the sun – either naturally or from tanning booths. You do need some sun, however (see chapter 18).

- Reduce stress (not always easy, I know). Psychological stress has been associated with oxidative damage.

- Reduce or eliminate alcohol.

- Reduce the total fat content of your diet. However, see chapters 13 and 14 on essential fats and oils.

- Try not to jog in areas of heavy traffic or in the rush hours. Moderate exercise reduces free radicals but overdoing exercise can produce more. Exercising daily or a few times a week is better than doing nothing all week then going mad at the weekend.

- Leading a sedentary lifestyle and having too much body fat can increase free radicals.

- Filter tap water or use glass bottled water.

- Try not to eat burnt or browned food. These contain free radicals. Burnt meat is especially bad.

- Keep nuts fresh. Nuts are good for us but can go off easily and it's not good to eat rancid nuts.

- Keep right away from processed oils (see chapter 24).

- Eat organic foods, as these are higher in antioxidants than non-organic foods.

In the following chapters, you will find foods that decrease oxidation although this is not the only way that they can help prevent cancer. Foods are extremely complicated and contain thousands of natural chemicals that can protect us from cancer in various different ways. I have named some of these chemicals throughout, but only a few to avoid filling the pages with long names.

CHAPTER 5

Breast cancer and insulin

Insulin is the hormone that helps glucose enter your cells. We need it and it is very important, but too much can have dangerous effects. This can cause all sorts of problems including type 2 diabetes. A study in the *Journal of Clinical Oncology* found that women with breast cancer whose fasting insulin levels were too high had poorer outcomes. People who suffer from diabetes appear to be more susceptible to breast cancer than those who do not. This is because higher levels of sugar in their blood lead to higher levels of insulin. Insulin causes breast cancer cells to divide in a similar way to oestrogen and oestrogen fuels most breast cancers. The more insulin there is in the blood, the more oestrogen. This is why it is so important to prevent it rising too high.

Insulin is associated with fat around the tummy area, the typical apple-shaped body with maybe slim legs and arms and reasonably-sized hips. Many women tend to look more like this as they get older. You can also see it in slim women who do not look fat but have an obvious tummy. Men can have what looks like a beer belly and beer has traditionally been blamed for this. Some men, however, have this shape without being beer drinkers. This is caused by diets high in sugar and refined carbohydrates.

Because some slim women can also have high levels of insulin, this is something to be aware of. In fact, I would recommend that all women have their insulin levels tested and, if it is too high, take steps to reduce it.

Insulin resistance

Some people cannot deal with insulin very well and are not efficient at metabolising it. The cells become resistant to it so it stays around in the bloodstream causing problems. In type 2 diabetes there is often enough insulin in the body but the cells have become resistant to it. This is related to the problem 'Syndrome X' where people suffer from fatigue, dizziness, weight gain and craving for sugar. It is also associated with polycystic ovary syndrome. In order to lower insulin you need a sensible diet.

Foods that raise insulin

Carbohydrates like sugar and starchy foods raise insulin. The fashion of eating a huge baked potato with very little protein is not good. Some high sugar fruit like bananas if eaten alone can also raise blood sugar and insulin to quite high levels in some people. Therefore, it is better to eat proper meals than sugary snacks. A wholemeal one slice bread sandwich with protein is much better than a white bread sandwich containing jam. The latter is almost pure sugar (apart from any butter on it). However, some would argue that any gluten grains like bread are not good.

Bread, rice, pasta and cereals are converted to glucose in the body. Some of these can raise insulin as much as sugar. You can see then that even eating a typical breakfast of toast, cereal, orange juice and stimulants like coffee is a very big sugar hit which can raise blood sugar very high with a corresponding rise in insulin. This chapter is written in conjunction with chapter 23 on sugar, which is one of the worst offenders regarding raising insulin.

How to lower insulin

- Eat frequent smaller meals of protein and complex carbohydrates. The combination of protein with carbohydrate makes the glucose in the carbohydrate enter the bloodstream at a slower rate as the protein is digested first.

- Include protein, some fat and some complex carbohydrates such as fruit or vegetables in your breakfast.

- Do not eat refined carbohydrates such as sweets, cakes, biscuits, white pasta, white bread and white rice. If you have had cancer, do not go mad with high sugar fruit.

- Be careful about certain complex carbohydrates like potatoes and bananas. These can also cause spikes in blood sugar, especially if eaten alone.

- Use spices that can lower blood sugar such as cinnamon, fenugreek, cloves, chives and garlic.

- Eat more high fibre foods (see chapter 15).

- Get enough sleep. Not sleeping produces high levels of the stress hormone, cortisol.

- Try to walk or do some good exercise for at least 30 minutes a day as exercise can lower insulin (see chapter 26 on this as exercise is extremely important).

CHAPTER 6

Foods that pack a punch

Carrots

Most people like carrots and they have always been a big part of the British diet. During World War Two they were even used to make jam. As a child, you may have been told that they can help you see in the dark. This is because they contain high levels of beta-carotene, which is converted to vitamin A. Vitamin A is needed for good eyesight. A typical British meal often consists of meat and two vegetables where one of the two is usually carrots. However, you may not know that carrots and other orange coloured fruit and vegetables are high in cancer-protecting substances called carotenoids. These compounds give fruit and vegetables their red and yellow colour. Amazingly, there are over 600 known carotenoids including alpha, beta and gamma-carotene.

Carotenoids are potent antioxidants, which your body needs to detoxify harmful chemicals. With regard to breast cancer, they promote something called cell differentiation. This just means that normal cells are all different from each other. For example, a brain cell is different from a blood cell and a skin cell is different from a bone cell. Different cells perform different tasks. However, cancer cells are not like that. They are all the same as each other and just grow in the body serving no useful purpose. Carotenoids in carrots and other coloured fruit and vegetables perform a useful function in helping to promote cell differentiation.

Carotenes

One particular carotenoid in carrots is beta-carotene, which can stimulate the body to produce natural killer (NK) cells. These are very important because their job is to hunt down and destroy cancer cells. Many studies have shown that a higher dietary intake of beta-carotene is related to a lower incidence of several cancers including breast cancer.

One large study called the 'Woman's Healthy Eating and Living Study' found that women with the highest concentration of carotenes in their blood were 43 per cent less likely to have a recurrence of breast cancer than those with the lowest levels. This was a large randomised controlled trial, which is often regarded as the gold standard of scientific research. This is where two groups of women are found and asked to eat different diets. One group was asked to eat a diet containing lots of fruit and vegetables, high fibre and low fat, and the other group was asked to eat a different diet that did not contain these foods. This is very good evidence that eating lots of fruit and vegetables is extremely protective.

Raw or cooked?

Many people ask if vegetables should be raw or cooked. I usually say that you should eat both, but if you can digest raw carrots you are in luck because they contain a chemical called falcarinol, which appear to be able to reduce cancer risk. This is good news for all those who like coleslaw or carrot grated into their salads.

However, some people do not digest raw vegetables very well. If you are one of those, do not worry as there is always carrot juice (but use a small amount mixed with other vegetable juices), and even cooked carrots have beneficial properties. In fact, studies using an artificial digestive system have found that the beta-carotene in carrots is better absorbed when the carrots have been cooked.

If you do not like carrots in any form, this is not a problem. Other carotenoids are found in large quantities in a variety of foods such as apricots, sweet potatoes, squash, watermelons and pink grapefruits. Funnily enough, dark green leafy vegetables also contain carotenoids but there the pink and red colours are disguised by the green cells, which contain a substance called chlorophyll.

Using carrots

There are so many ways to use carrots. You can include them in soups and stews and you can use grated carrot in salads or sandwiches. Carrot juice has often been recommended by naturopaths for people with cancer. However, if you are going to make this juice, I suggest that you use just a small amount of carrot and more green vegetables such as celery and cucumber. This is because carrots are high in natural sugars and you do not want to overload your system and cause spikes in blood sugar.

Carrots can be combined with spices to make exotic Middle Eastern-tasting dishes. For something different, try adding turmeric and cinnamon. We will discuss later the fact that fermented foods are very protective and it is possible to ferment carrots along with cabbage and other vegetables.

Sweet potatoes

Funnily enough, sweet potatoes are not potatoes at all. They are part of a very different family with the lovely name of 'morning glory'. Despite their name, sweet potatoes are less likely to raise blood sugar than white potatoes even though they actually taste quite sweet. They are also high in carotenoids, as are pumpkins, winter squash, apricots, mangoes, cantaloupe melons and tomatoes. The purple variety is also high in alpha-carotene, which has even better anti-cancer properties due to the anthocyanidins in the purple pigment. Eating a large variety of different vegetables gives us more of the anti-cancer properties that can help us.

Okra

This is a vegetable which is not very common in the UK, but a very recent study has shown that it was able to inhibit the growth of cancer cells in test tubes by 63 per cent. Originally from Africa it is used in Caribbean, Creole, Cajun and Indian cuisine.

Celery

Celery is a food that has many fans, including me. There is so much that you can do with celery to provide interesting and nutritious meals. It has long been used to help lower blood pressure but the latest research has found that it can also be useful in the prevention of breast cancer.

Celery contains an interesting chemical called apigenin, which has been shown to be protective. One study was carried out on mice that were implanted with a deadly, fast-growing human breast cancer. When they were given apigenin, the growth of the cancer slowed down and the tumour shrank. The blood vessels bringing food and oxygen to the tumour also shrank and the tumour reduced because of starvation. Apigenin is also found in broccoli, tomatoes, cherries and tea.

You may know that women who have been treated for oestrogen-positive breast cancer are given the drug letrozole after treatment. This drug stops the body converting male hormones to oestrogen. The body does this by way of an enzyme called aromatase. Amazingly, an Italian population study has found that apigenin has a modest ability to inhibit the aromatase enzyme and that the risk of breast cancer is reduced with the consumption of celery.

Using celery

- Include in vegetable soups and stews.

- Make a Waldorf salad with small pieces of celery, chopped apple, walnuts and a small amount of crumbled blue cheese.

- Use for dips.

- Make juices with celery, cucumber and a small carrot.

Parsley

This herb also contains high levels of apigenin and is a good way to garnish many dishes. It adds colour and flavour to soups and stews. Parsley is antioxidant and anti-inflammatory and contains a chemical called luteolin, which can inhibit the growth of oestrogen-negative breast cancer cells. It is also a rich source of vitamin K, needed for healthy bones.

Using parsley

- Sprinkle chopped parsley before serving in soups and stews.

- Add as a garnish on many dishes.

- Mix together bulgur wheat, chopped mint and chopped parsley to make tabbouleh.

Rosemary

Rosemary is another herb which also has breast cancer protective properties. It appears to be very powerful in reducing inflammation and can help our liver detoxify dangerous chemicals. Interestingly, it can also stop these chemicals binding to our DNA.

Rosemary can be drunk as a tea and the leaves can be used in cooking in almost any food. A novel idea is to use rosemary sticks as skewers for kebab-type dishes.

Seaweeds or sea vegetables

Seaweed might not be the first thing that comes to mind when we think of protecting ourselves from breast cancer. However, studies have shown that it has potent anti-cancer properties. This is because it is so high in iodine and iodine can be toxic to breast cancer cells. It can also help our body produce antioxidants and is necessary for the correct functioning of the thyroid gland. There seems to be a relationship between this and breast cancer. It appears that women with thyroid conditions such as hypothyroid, hyperthyroid, goitres and thyroiditis (inflammation of the thyroid) are more likely to get breast cancer.

Of all the seaweeds that exist, and there are many, the one that the UK would recognise is kelp. This shiny brown substance has bubbles that children love to pop. You can see it on beaches all over Britain. Its proper name is 'laminaria' but we would be more likely to call it 'kelp'. You can buy kelp tablets in health food shops, but do not take it from the beach and eat it.

Breast cancer and sea vegetables

For the prevention of breast cancer, an important study was carried out at the University of California, Berkeley where they found that giving rats a diet containing kelp lowered levels of the hormone oestradiol in their bodies. This hormone is one of the three that make up the oestrogen group and is the most likely to cause breast cancer.

Women in Japan eat quite a lot of kelp, which makes up 10 per cent of their diet. The level of breast cancer is much lower than in Europe and the lowest rates are in the rural towns where seaweed is eaten at every meal. Although that is just a correlation and does not prove this is the cause, other studies support it. When researchers looked at oestradiol in rats, they found that feeding them kelp reduced it from 48.9 nanograms per litre to 36.7 nanograms per litre after four weeks. Another study published in the *Japanese Journal of Cancer Research* found that the seaweed wakame suppressed the growth of breast cancer tumours implanted into rats. If you do not like fish, therefore, you could take a good supplement of kelp as a source of iodine. This needs to be toxin-free so choose a reputable company.

CHAPTER 7
Jolly green giants

Children are usually urged to eat their greens and this is often highly resisted. Many are told that they are 'good for you' but it was not known until recently how good they actually are. We now know that green vegetables contain plant chemicals that can do a wonderful and unique job in preventing cancers of all kinds. The exciting thing for us is that these foods are actually top of the league for the prevention of breast cancer in particular. The reason for this is that chemicals in these foods have the unique ability to protect us from the damaging effects of oestrogen.

Cruciferous vegetables

The most important green vegetables for the prevention of breast cancer are called cruciferous vegetables or vegetables from the brassica family. They are called cruciferous because there is a distinctive cross shape on the flower. Cruciferous vegetables or crucifers include cabbage, broccoli, cauliflower, Brussels sprouts, kohlrabi, collards, savoy cabbage, watercress and kale. Strangely enough, radishes and turnips are also part of this family, even though they are not green.

In ancient times, these vegetables were grown mainly for medicinal purposes and they still pack a punch today. The Romans in particular saw cabbage as being very important for healing and in fact, cabbage leaves were sometimes put on breast tumours to try to help them.

Today many studies show that cruciferous vegetables are the most protective of all the vegetables for breast cancer. This is because they have unique properties not found in other foods. One study in particular found that women who ate the most cruciferous vegetables had a 40 per cent lower risk of breast cancer than those who ate the least. Although this was just one study, another paper, which was written after a review of 13 different studies, concluded that eating cruciferous vegetables could indeed reduce the risk of breast cancer.

Of cabbages and kings

Cabbage is certainly fit for kings and for anyone else who wants to protect their health. It was first cultivated 6,000 years ago and may be our oldest farmed vegetable. There are many types of cabbage including red cabbage where the red pigment affords the vegetable even more anti-cancer properties. However, all cabbage is antioxidant and anti-inflammatory and can help us in many ways. In particular, it contains glucosinolates that break down into indoles – one of which is sulforaphane. Another is indole-3-carbinol, formed when these vegetables are cooked or crushed.

It is because it contains indole-3-carbinol that cabbage is particularly valuable for the prevention of breast cancer. This chemical is very clever as it has more than one function in the body and can help prevent breast cancer in various different ways.

One amazing thing that it does is to change 'bad' oestrogen to 'good' oestrogen in the liver. Oestrogen is not of one type. There are actually many different types, the main ones being oestriol, oestrone and oestradiol. Oestriol is the weakest and the least likely to be associated with breast cancer. The good and amazing thing about indole-3-carbinol is that it can change oestradiol to the more benign form. This function is unique in the food world and is very important. In fact, at least one study found that women with breast cancer have almost twice as much 'bad' oestrogen in their bodies as 'good' oestrogen.

Another way that indole-3-carbinol works is through the breast cell receptors. If this chemical is present when oestrogen tries to attach to breast cells, the cells do not divide as fast as usual.

Therefore, cabbage is one of our most protective foods against breast cancer so try to eat it most days. The best way to prepare cabbage is not to have it soggy and over-cooked. It is better to eat it lightly cooked or raw to preserve its enzymes. You could sauté it lightly or stir-fry it, but do not microwave it.

Broccoli

If you are not keen on broccoli, you are not the only one. George Bush is reported as saying that he hates it. His exact words were, 'I do not like broccoli. I have not liked it since I was a little kid and my mother made me eat it. In addition, I am President of the United States and I am not going to eat any more broccoli!'

Broccoli, however, is a powerhouse of anti-cancer chemicals and if you like it, or can get to like it, you will be going a long way to protecting yourself from breast cancer. It contains an important chemical called sulforaphane. Studies in test tubes have shown that it can prevent cancer cells proliferating and cause them to self-destruct. It also helps neutralise cancer-causing substances in the liver. In fact, it is so useful for cancer prevention that scientists at Johns Hopkins University in the United States are actually trying to develop synthetic forms of this powerful chemical. However, you do not need to wait until that happens. You can eat broccoli now and gain all the protection that it contains. Another very important benefit is that, like cabbage, it is rich in indole-3-carbinol. It is also high in calcium so it is good for those who do not eat dairy products.

Broccoli sprouts

If you really cannot bear to eat broccoli (or even if you can), you can always turn to broccoli sprouts. These do not taste like broccoli but are even more effective in preventing cancer. They contain 20 to 50 times as much sulforaphane as mature broccoli. Just 5g of sprouts contain the same number of protective chemicals as 150g of broccoli. They are easy to grow and look and taste a little like alfalfa sprouts.

To grow them, use organic seeds and put one tablespoon in a glass jar. Fill half of the jar with water. Get some netting or gauze and attach to the top of the jar with a rubber band. Leave the seeds for two hours and then drain the water. Rinse the seeds twice a day. You can eat them after about three days. Once sprouted, they will stay fresh for a week if kept in the fridge in an airtight container. One pound of broccoli sprouts is equal to 40 pounds of fresh broccoli. They are easy to make.

Cauliflower

Even though this is a pale white vegetable, it is still one of the best sources of anti-cancer chemicals around. Like other cruciferous vegetables it contains indole-3-carbinol, is high in antioxidants and is a very good source of vitamin K, needed for healthy bones. While cauliflower is usually white, there is also a purple variety, which is high in cancer-preventing anthocyanins similar to those in red wine and red cabbage. Cauliflower is a very adaptable vegetable with its mild tastes and knobbly texture.

Using cruciferous vegetables

We all know about the British meat-and-two-veg dinners that were eaten in the UK in the past and still are today. One of the two veg was often cabbage, sometimes quite soggy and often swimming in pools of water. I do not mind this way of eating cabbage but I can understand that other people might not be too enamoured by it. However, there are many other ways to eat cabbage, which might be more appetising. In any case, it is better to eat cabbage raw or lightly steamed to preserve all the health-giving properties than trying to plough your way through the soggy preparations.

- Make coleslaw with chopped cabbage, grated carrots and a tiny amount of mayonnaise. This takes a couple of minutes in a food processor.

- Mix cabbage with cooked potato to make the delicious Irish dish, colcannon.

- Add cabbage and other cruciferous vegetables to soups and stews.

- Make pickled cabbage (see chapter 19 on fermented foods).

- If you love pizza, use a very thin base and load up the topping with lots of vegetables including broccoli.

- Make borscht, a traditional beetroot and cabbage soup, which combines the green pigments of cabbage with the health-giving red pigments of beetroot.

- Add cooked or raw broccoli to rice, salads or pasta dishes.

- Add broccoli sprouts to sandwiches.

- Make cauliflower cheese – a British favourite for a long time.

- Sauté cauliflower in olive oil and add curry powder.

- Try adding cauliflower to soups as a thickener.

- Try making a cauliflower pizza crust, if you are sensitive to wheat. There are many recipes on the Internet.

Watercress

Though not a crucifer, watercress also has anti-cancer properties. It is a strong-tasting green vegetable that adds interest to salads. It contains the important antioxidant phenethyl isothiocyanate. Research at the University of Southampton has found that it can suppress the development of cancer cells. It does this by turning off signals for the tumour to get a blood supply. A study at the University of Ulster has also found that it could reduce damage to DNA.

Watercress adds crunch and taste to just about anything and is light and easy to use. Add it to omelettes, pizzas and sandwiches.

CHAPTER 8
Not an animal or a plant

Do you like mushrooms? I hope you do because mushrooms have many health-giving properties. Because of this, they have been used for medicinal purposes for thousands of years. The odd thing about mushrooms is that they are neither plant nor animal. They are actually fungi and at present about a hundred different species are being studied for their health-giving properties. Fortunately for us, this tasty food contains hundreds of chemicals including some that support our immune systems and can help prevent cancer.

At present, there are 32 human clinical trials being carried out in the United States looking for ways in which mushrooms help our health. In one case-control study, though not a trial, 358 Korean women with breast cancer were matched with a group of women with no cancer. The study found that pre-menopausal women who ate more mushrooms were less likely to get breast cancer than those who ate fewer.

Although the above was a single study, similar results have been found in other studies and also in reviews. Reviews are very valuable because they give the overall results of many different types of research, which add to their credibility. A very recent review of ten studies (eight case-control and two cohort studies) looked at 6,870 women with breast cancer and compared them with healthy women. They found that for both pre-menopausal and post-menopausal women, those who ate mushrooms were less likely to get cancer than those who did not.

There are many types of mushrooms. Some are very exotic and therefore quite expensive, so scientists wanted to find out which were the best for cancer prevention. To do this they placed cancer cells in test tubes with mushrooms of different sorts: maitake (grifola), crimini, portobello, oyster and white button mushrooms. They were pleased to find that all of the mushrooms tested stopped the cancer cells growing. Maitake mushrooms in particular were very interesting because they also caused the cancer cells to self-destruct. Incidentally, an extract of one mushroom was found to kill 95 per cent of prostate cancer cells within 24 hours.

Lowering oestrogen

Some mushrooms are quite exotic and quite expensive but, thankfully, the study mentioned on the previous page showed that the common white mushroom is very valuable for cancer protection, and in the UK it can be bought very easily and cheaply. In fact, it was found to be the best aromatase inhibitor of all the mushrooms tested, suppressing the aromatase enzyme in a dose-dependent way. This means that the higher the amount used, the less aromatase activity there was.

Aromatase inhibitors stop male hormones in a woman's body being converted to oestrogen. We have seen that after menopause a woman's ovaries do not produce much oestrogen but the male hormones that she has can be turned into oestrogen by the enzyme aromatase.

How to use mushrooms

Mushrooms are quite versatile and can be used in all sorts of dishes. Mushroom risotto is a favourite with many. To make this, just add cooked mushrooms to rice along with some vegetables. There is no need to stick to the usual onions for this dish. Add on any other vegetables you like to increase the anti-cancer properties.

Mushroom soup is also very easy to make. Just sauté the mushrooms with onion, add water and simmer, then use a hand blender to blend the lot. You can make it thicker or thinner just by varying the amount of water you use.

Mushroom omelettes are tasty, and of course mushrooms on toast are really delicious and easy to prepare. Finely chopped cooked mushrooms can be sprinkled on salads and used in soups and stews. Add them also to small baked potatoes. For those who really do not like mushrooms, supplements are available but it is better to use fresh mushrooms if you can.

Mushrooms need to be cooked as most varieties contain some toxins which are usually destroyed by cooking.

Maitake MD-fraction

An extract of the maitake mushroom has apparently been found to have greater anti-cancer properties than extracts of other mushrooms. In laboratory tests on animals, researchers have found that this extract – Maitake MD-fraction – can stimulate white blood cells. These cells are called 'macrophages', which means big eaters, and they work by engulfing or 'eating' foreign particles like cancer cells. Maitake MD-fraction can be bought in capsule form.

Better together

We have already discussed the value of eating foods together and this is borne out by a study of women in China published in the *International Journal of Cancer*. This was an attempt to look at the effect of mushrooms alone and mushrooms with green tea. It compared women with breast cancer aged 20-87 with healthy women with no breast cancer. They found that the healthy women in general who ate more mushrooms had less breast cancer (both pre- and post-menopausal women). However, if they also drank green tea, there was a further decrease in risk. So why not have a cup of green tea with meals containing mushrooms?

How much do we need?

There would be little point in knowing that mushrooms can prevent tumour growth if we had to eat vast quantities of them to have an effect. Fortunately, however, an anti-cancer effect can apparently be brought about by eating just 100g.

CHAPTER 9
Amazing alliums

The onion family includes onions, garlic, leeks, chives, shallots and scallions. This is actually a very large family as it contains about 500 different species. These certainly can pack a punch when it comes to our health. Studies from around the world have shown that a higher intake of these vegetables is associated with a reduced risk of several types of cancer. In particular, it has been found that those who consume plenty of them are less likely to suffer from breast cancer.

Garlic

Garlic is an amazing food. How many different plant chemicals do you think it contains? The answer is over 200 as far as is known. It is an extremely complex food and it can be a great addition to your cancer-prevention arsenal. Garlic has been known as a special food for thousands of years. In fact, when the pyramids were being built, workers were given a clove of garlic a day, and, in the First World War, soldiers' wounds were treated with garlic to prevent infection. Garlic is anti-inflammatory, anti-arthritic, antiseptic, anti-fungal and can lower blood fats like cholesterol and triglycerides.

It is also known to have anti-cancer properties that can halt the growth of tumours of the digestive system such as stomach and colon cancers and also prostate cancer. We are discussing prevention here and not treatment. But what can it do for preventing breast cancer? Evidence that garlic can protect against breast cancer has not been as forthcoming as with other cancers. However, very recent studies have shown that it does have anti-cancer properties and that garlic-derived compounds can reduce the development of breast cancer in animals and kill breast cancer cells in vitro (in test tubes). One study concluded by saying that it might be 'a useful food in the control of breast cancer'. Another study found that garlic was able to make breast cancer cells self-destruct. One important function of garlic is that it can stop nitrates in foods like sausages being changed in the body to the dangerous, cancer-causing chemicals, nitrosamines.

Studies have also shown that it can increase the numbers of natural killer cells in the body. This is important for us as these protect us in very complex and valuable ways. Sadly, as well as killing cancer cells in the laboratory, it could also kill your friendships if your friends get a whiff of it! If you are worried about your breath smelling, try chewing it with some parsley as this can help. Otherwise you can use supplements, although I do think that the real thing is better.

Onions

Louis Pasteur was the first to identify the antibacterial properties of onion and garlic. Onions are extremely useful in cooking and very protective to the body. The red and yellow varieties are rich in a substance called quercetin, which has been called 'the king of the flavonoids'. It boosts the immune system, reduces inflammation and helps your liver deal with toxic substances. It is a strange fact that many pregnant women seem to crave pickled onions.

Research in China found that those who consumed the most garlic, scallions, chives and onions had a 40 per cent reduction in the rate of stomach cancer. Onions are also able to protect us from breast cancer. A systematic review, looking at evidence from different Swiss and Italian studies, found that women who ate the most onions had a 25 per cent reduced risk of breast cancer. This was a case-control study where those with breast cancer were compared to those who were healthy. Although this type of study does not prove a causal relationship, another study of breast cancer cells in vitro found that onion extract was able to make them self-destruct.

Using alliums

- Add chopped raw onion to salads and sandwiches.

- Make a tasty dish with grated hard-boiled egg, chopped onion and a very tiny bit of salad cream.

- Use onions and garlic in all soups and stews.

- Make onion tarts.

- Try French onion soup.

- Add onions and a little garlic to omelettes and scrambled eggs.

- Chives or spring onions can be chopped and used in potato salad.

CHAPTER 10

Fantastic fruits

Citrus fruits

Citrus fruits are refreshing and delicious. Most people are aware that they also contain high levels of vitamin C. Fortunately for us they also have anti-cancer properties including 60 polyphenols. According to the American National Cancer Institute, oranges are 'a complete package of every class of natural anti-cancer inhibitor known'. Even the peel of citrus fruits contains the cancer protector, limonene. One study found that those who ate more citrus peel had less skin cancer. Having said that, I cannot imagine that the thought of eating citrus peel is making you eager to go and try some. But do not worry – the whole fruit is just as beneficial, and is much more pleasant to eat than the peel.

A high intake of citrus fruits has been found to be associated with a 10 per cent reduction in breast cancer according to one systematic review. This is where many different studies are discussed and the author looks for overall results. Over 8,000 women were included in this particular review.

In another study of 3,000 women, those who ate the most citrus fruits had a 32 per cent reduction in the risk of breast cancer compared to those who ate the least. This supports the results of other research carried out in test tubes. One of these studies found that two chemicals in citrus fruits, hesperidin and naringenin, stopped the growth of breast cancer cells, especially when combined with quercetin from other foods.

Eating foods together

As we have seen, combining different foods together enhances their cancer-protective properties. It has been found that quercetin in onions is a very important cancer-protective substance, so why not have a glass of orange juice with a meal containing onions?

Lemons

Lemons are tangy and refreshing and they also contain cancer-protective chemicals. Some of these are limonoids, of which there are many. In one laboratory study, it was found that 11 of these were toxic to breast cancer cells and seven were toxic to both oestrogen-positive breast cells as well as oestrogen-negative cells. Another good thing about limonoids is that, in high concentrations, they have the ability to block the aromatase enzyme, which the body uses to convert a woman's male hormones to oestrogen.

Another study tested various different types of limonoids and concluded that, 'Our findings indicated that the citrus limonoids may have potential for the prevention of oestrogen-responsive breast cancer...' Limonoids are not just found in lemons but also in other citrus fruits.

Here again, combining different foods has been found to be beneficial. Consuming citrus fruits with green tea reduces the risk of breast cancer by 26 per cent, so why not squeeze some real lemon juice into your green tea instead of buying the flavoured variety. It is interesting that drinking tea with a slice of lemon has been done for hundreds of years by traditional societies. They obviously knew things then that we could learn from, and that are now being proven scientifically. This seems to happen time and time again.

Ways to use lemons

We might not feel that we can use lemons widely due to their sour taste but below are a few ideas.

- Add lemon juice instead of vinegar to extra virgin olive oil for a pleasant tasting salad dressing or just squeeze it straight onto salads.
- Make a hot lemon drink with a little honey.
- Make a light and refreshing lemon sorbet.
- Serve a slice of lemon to squeeze over fish dishes or even meat.

- Add lemon juice to green tea to help the beneficial chemicals (catechins) to work.

Pomegranates

Pomegranates are delicious, juicy fruits which have been studied extensively in relation to prostate cancer. Many studies show that they are also beneficial for the prevention of breast cancer. They contain substances called luteolin, ellagic acid and punicic acid, which can stop breast cancer cells migrating to the bones. This is very important for women who have had breast cancer already.

Another way that pomegranates can affect cancer is to do with oestrogen. One study concluded that 'pomegranate ET-derived compounds have potential for the prevention of oestrogen-responsive breast cancer'. As we have seen with some other foods, they do this by their effect on the enzyme that converts male hormones to oestrogen (aromatase). Drugs like letrozole which are given to post-menopausal breast cancer survivors to lower oestrogen also work in this way.

The oil from the seeds in pomegranates has also been found to be effective. One study showed that this oil caused an 87 per cent reduction in the proliferation of cancer cells in vitro. They also found that it was able to reduce the production of new blood vessels in the tumour itself.

Personally, I find the seeds of pomegranates difficult to eat but it seems that the oil from these seeds has better protective value than the juice alone. It is now possible to buy cartons of pomegranate seeds on their own. When buying pomegranates, look for ones that are rather brown and off-colour, as strangely enough, they tend to be sweeter.

How to use pomegranates

- Sprinkle on salads, desserts and yogurt.

- Make an interesting hors d'oeuvres with melon chunks and fresh mint – great for hot summer evenings.

- Make a salad with lettuce, pecans, blue cheese, pear slices and pomegranate seeds.

- Use the seeds as a garnish on just about anything to add interest, colour and flavour.

- Dilute the juice, if drinking it on its own, in order to prevent too high a rise in blood sugar.

Berries

Berries really are superfoods. Not only delicious, they are also higher in plant chemicals and other anti-cancer compounds than most other fruits. Their rich dark blue colour (along with the reds, pinks, blacks, mauves and purples) shows you that they contain important chemicals called anthocyanins, ellagic acid and proanthocyanidins of which there are over 150 in the plant world. They are also high in other antioxidants. In fact, fruits with blue, black and purple pigments have the highest antioxidant values of all fruit.

One study concludes that, 'Overwhelming evidence suggests that edible small and soft-fleshed berry fruits may have beneficial effects against several types of human cancers.' Other research has shown that they can reduce and even repair damage done by oxidation and inflammation. They are also low in sugar compared to other fruits, so are less likely to affect insulin levels or cause weight gain. When buying berries, it is important to choose organic.

Cherries

These have become much more common in shops recently and that is good because cherries are rich in protective chemicals. Like blueberries, they are rich in anthocyanidens, which have several anti-cancer effects. One study found that breast cancer cells were able to self-destruct (apoptosis) when left in a solution of tart cherry juice. They are rich in perillyl alcohol, a compound related to limonene in citrus fruits, but they are five times more powerful. For cancer prevention, sour cherries have been studied more than the sweet variety. Interestingly, another condition which can be helped by cherries is gout.

Blueberries

Blueberries are one of the few fruits that are native to North America and songs have been written about their famous blueberry pie. They are a very low sugar fruit and taste just great. Children love them and younger children can easily pick them up with small fingers. They are one of the healthiest fruits on earth and a great way to protect you from illness. The dark blue/black pigments in blueberries are rich in phenols and this is why blueberries are one of the fruits highest in antioxidants.

Studies in mice have shown that blueberries can be helpful in triple negative breast cancer, which accounts for about 15 per cent of breast cancers. Female mice with breast tumours were given a high fat diet typical of that eaten in modern Western societies, plus 5 per cent whole blueberry powder. It was found that the mice given the powder had significantly smaller tumours, less ulceration and less metastasis to the lymph nodes than mice fed a Western diet. They also showed higher levels of anti-inflammatory substances in their blood. There was no effect on normal cells. Another study found that when a 5 per cent blueberry extract was given to mice they developed 70 per cent fewer metastases to the liver and lymph nodes compared to the control group.

An important chemical in blueberries is delphinidin. Interestingly, this is the pigment that gives the red-blue colour to the grapes that make the famous Cabernet Sauvignon wine. One laboratory study found that delphinidin in blueberries can inhibit activity of the vascular endothelial growth factor (VEGF) receptor. VEGF is a chemical that helps to produce new blood vessels, enabling cancerous cells to grow and proliferate. Cancerous cells cannot grow more than a few millimetres without a blood supply to bring them the oxygen and nutrients they need.

Blueberries also contain proanthocyanidins which may be able to stop your body making oestrogen. They also help reduce inflammation, reduce damage to DNA and make cancer cells self-destruct.

Raspberries

Raspberries are part of the rose family and there are over 200 species. The red-purple colour in berries like these comes from anthocyanins. Another phytochemical in raspberries called ellagic acid was found to stop the growth of breast cancer cells in test tubes. As with blueberries, this fruit can also inhibit the activity of VEGF. Drug companies are trying to manufacture anti-VEGF drugs so it's amazing that we can experience the benefits without any side effects by eating these natural foods.

Bilberries

Bilberries, known as blaeberries in Scotland, are renowned for their ability to protect the eyes, but studies have shown that they can also be protective of the breasts. Laboratory studies have shown that they can inhibit the proliferation of breast cancer cells and cause them to self-destruct. It is rather odd that, although they are native to Britain, and blueberries are not, it is much easier to find blueberries for sale in the UK than bilberries.

Blackberries

In Scotland these are called 'brambles' and I spent many happy hours picking these when I was a child. Even then, my father warned me about picking those on the main roads where the pollution from cars might contaminate them. This is even more important today. So if you go berry picking, choose a quiet spot with no cars passing. Blackberries also have the dark coloured blue-black pigments that are rich in antioxidants. One study found that the Hull variety of blackberries have antioxidant and anti-inflammatory actions and may have potential for the prevention of cancer.

Black raspberries

These are very high in ellagic acid – higher than any other berry studied. Apparently, compounds in black raspberries can slow down the rate of growth of cells that could become cancerous and can cause those cells to die.

Strawberries

Strawberries have an unusual feature for fruit in that their seeds are on the outside of the fruit instead of the inside. This is why you can easily make a drawing or a painting of a strawberry instantly recognisable by putting black dots on the red strawberry colour. Although research has suggested that strawberries can help prevent other cancers, the evidence for the prevention of breast cancer is mixed.

Ways to use berries

- In yogurt.

- In pies and muffins.

- In smoothies blended with other fruits.

- In sorbets.

- In ice lollies – blend some and freeze.

- In fruit salad.

- In hors d'oeuvres: smoked salmon, mint leaves, melon chunks and blueberries.

- Freeze blueberries and use all year round.

Peaches and plums

The very latest research has found that peaches can stop breast cancer cells growing and spreading to other organs. A study at the Texas A&M University found that when cancer cells were implanted into mice they did not grow or get into the bloodstream if the mice were given peaches beforehand. Even the most aggressive cells died. Peaches contain polyphenols and it is these that are the active ingredients. Polyphenols are antioxidants but the antioxidants are not the only chemicals that are responsible for the anti-cancer effect. Polyphenols work in many complex ways. Plants use them to protect themselves against heat and pathogens. Fortunately, we can use them too as a very pleasant way to protect ourselves from cancer.

It is important to eat peaches fresh rather than cooked and, as the polyphenols are concentrated on the skin, we should eat that too. You might be wondering how many you should eat a day. The research shows that two or three would be a reasonable amount. Three to me seems a lot. A better option would be to eat a couple and then add on a variety of other fruit.

Peaches are related to the very nutritious plums, of which there are around 2,000 different varieties. Like peaches, plums are high in polyphenols and extracts of this fruit have been found to decrease the proliferation of breast cancer cells. As you might expect, darker coloured plums are higher in antioxidants than the lighter ones and the skin is richer than the flesh.

Prunes

As you saw from the antioxidant table, prunes come way up high on the list. You might have expected this from their dark blue/black pigments. Prunes are actually dried plums and you can buy soft squishy ones without juice. They are good if you feel like something sweet. Be careful, though, as it is easy to eat too many without thinking as they are quite small and tempting. Because they are dried, they are very concentrated, especially in fruit sugar, so eating too many all at one time could give you quite a high sugar fix. They are also known to relieve constipation so that is another reason not to eat too many.

Lychees

Lychees are less common in the UK but those who visit Chinese restaurants may have tasted them and found them delicious. They are a little like white grapes with a large stone in the centre. They contain flavonoids such as quercetin and appear from in vitro studies to be especially effective against breast cancer cells.

Pineapple

This is a delicious tasting fruit and wonderful to include in fruit salads. However, you may not know that it also contains anti-cancer properties. One of the most important ingredients in pineapple is bromelain. This is sometimes taken as a supplement to reduce inflammation. Bromelain is an enzyme that helps to digest protein. Laboratory studies have shown that it can make cancer cells self-destruct, especially breast cancer cells. It can also dissolve the coating that tumours build around themselves to protect them from the immune system. They do this with a substance called fibrin. Because bromelain is an enzyme, it can digest fibrin. In fact, some natural therapists recommend taking protein-digesting enzymes between meals to do just this.

A study on animals carried out by Dr Tracy Mynott at Queensland Institute of Medical Research in Australia found that tumour growth could be greatly inhibited with bromelain. Remember that in this book we are talking about prevention rather than treatment and the idea is to prevent microscopic tumours gaining a foothold.

It is best to eat pineapple away from protein foods because otherwise it will be used up digesting the protein. It is often a good idea to eat fruit between meals anyway because if you eat it with meals it can take too long to digest. This makes it sit in the stomach and ferment, causing wind and bloating. Do not eat too much pineapple as it is very sweet and can raise insulin levels.

Apples

Most of us grew up with apples and dishes made from them. Some of you may have had apple trees in your garden and enjoyed the small sour fruits that they produced. Apples may be ordinary but they are not simple. They actually contain more anti-cancer properties than some of the more exotic fruits described in this chapter. Studies have found that the peel of the apple contains exceptionally high levels of valuable antioxidants. This is why it is such a pity that many people just throw it away. One study published in the journal *Nutrition and Cancer* found that peel extract from organic Gala apples possessed strong anti-proliferative effects against cancer cells. The study advised that the peels should not be discarded.

Adding spices to apples can make them even more protective. Cinnamon and cloves have traditionally been used to flavour apple pies and baked apples. Add antioxidant-rich raisins to sweeten them rather than sugar. All of these make the food smell wonderful and taste even better.

Combine them again

If you enjoy drinking smoothies, this is very good because as we have seen earlier, combining fruits increases the antioxidant power of the foods by more than just the sum of the fruits themselves. Mixing different berries in smoothies is a simple and nutritious way to do this. You can include whatever fruits you like. On the other hand, I do not recommend drinking shop-bought smoothies, as they are often high in cheaper fruits or thickening fruits like bananas, while describing themselves as berry smoothies. It is better to make them yourself with a blending jug. These jugs are cheap to buy, convenient to use and easy to clean.

Although I recommend drinking smoothies, it is not a good idea to drink undiluted fruit juice. This is because smoothies contain the whole fruit with all the fibre intact, the way we were meant to eat fruit. Fruit juices do not contain fibre. Therefore, they are digested immediately. This can raise your blood sugar too high, too quickly. If you do not like smoothies, you could still get the synergistic effect by eating fruit salad instead. Ready-cut fruits are useful for lunches and can be found in most supermarkets.

CHAPTER 11
Organic food

Organic food has become more popular over the years and this is a good thing. Some people might argue that it is a waste of money and that there is nothing wrong with ordinary non-organic food. This is not the case. Many different chemicals are allowed on our food, and we cannot know for definite what combinations of these are doing in our bodies.

Non-organic food is grown with the use of pesticides, which include insecticides to kill insects, herbicides to kill weeds and fungicides to kill fungal conditions. Some of these stay on the plant and some are carcinogenic. One study looked at the concentration of organochlorine pesticides found in blood and the risk of prostate cancer and found that there was an association. With regard to breast cancer, results have been inconsistent, especially relating to concentrations in the blood. However, when breast tissue itself has been looked at, some studies have shown that there is an association between organochlorines from pesticides and breast cancer. A study in the journal *Breast Cancer Research* concluded that these pesticides found in the fatty tissue in the breast create an oestrogenic environment in that area.

We do know that organochlorines are also concentrated and stored in the body fat of the animals that we eat. Vegetables too are tainted with pesticides. In the words of breast cancer surgeon Dr Christine Horner, 'A sample of conventionally grown celery was found to contain seventeen different pesticide residues, ten of which were carcinogenic.' These chemicals can act like oestrogen in the body and that is why they are called xenoestrogens or foreign oestrogens.

What exactly is organic food?
Organic food means food grown without artificial chemical fertilisers. Pesticides are severely restricted and antibiotics and other drugs are

not used as routine. In addition to this, organic farmers do not grow genetically modified crops.

It is natural for plants to be exposed to attack by insects. They defend themselves by way of protease inhibitors, which stunt the growth of the insects and prevent them consuming much of the plant. If one leaf has been attacked, the whole plant increases levels of this chemical to protect itself. This is the wonder of nature! Protease inhibitors protect us from cancer and organic food has more of them.

In the past, all food was grown organically. However, apart from the dangers of non-organic food, is organic food higher in nutrients? The latest research has shown that it is. One review of 343 peer-reviewed publications found that levels of antioxidants were substantially higher in organic crops. If pesticides are used, plants do not need to produce antioxidants to defend themselves. In addition to this, pesticide residues were four times higher than in the organic food and these contained higher levels of toxic cadmium.

Another reason for buying organic food when on a high vegetable diet is that there is not much point in consuming all the antioxidants in plant foods if you are going to ingest even more pesticides than you did before.

Even if you do buy organic food, you need to wash it carefully, especially if grown on manure, and health food shops sell special solutions for doing this. Of course, you can always grow some vegetables yourself if you have a spare patch in the garden.

Organic livestock

Many cancer-prevention writers recommend not eating meat or chicken at all. However, if you cannot do that entirely or if you choose to eat some meat or chicken, it should be a small amount. It could be there on the plate to add taste and interest rather than being the centrepiece of the meal. It should also be organic. Although organic meat can be expensive, by having smaller amounts and eating it less often, you may find that the extra cost is small.

Ordinary chickens in particular can have a very hard life. They are often dosed with steroids and antibiotics and kept in poor conditions. Who knows what they are fed? I buy only organic chicken and do not eat it often. Free range just means that the chickens can move about freely. However, they are not necessarily fed differently from ordinary chickens. All organic chicken is free range but not all free range is organic.

With other meat, farmers move the livestock around more and keep smaller herds in order to prevent them from getting diseases.

CHAPTER 12

What to drink?
Make your tea green

What is nicer than sitting down and relaxing with a nice cup of tea? In the UK this has traditionally been black tea, but other teas such as green tea are now becoming quite popular. Tea has been a well-loved drink for thousands of years and green tea in particular is a favourite drink in the Far East. It has been drunk in Asia for over 3,000 years and is still very popular today. Green tea always makes me think of happy evenings in Chinese restaurants. It is so light, so refreshing and tastes exotic. However, green tea is not just a pleasant drink. Who would have thought that it could be such a powerful friend in helping to prevent breast cancer? It is a powerhouse of cancer-fighting chemicals and there is ample research to back this up.

Green tea and breast cancer

One study of 74,000 Chinese women found that regularly drinking green tea could delay the onset of breast cancer. From an analysis of 13 different studies which looked at populations in eight countries, it was apparent that those who drank green tea had a much lower risk of getting breast cancer than those who did not. This is not proof in itself but other types of research have come to the same conclusion. Vitamins C and E are important antioxidants but the antioxidants in green tea are 100 times more effective than vitamin C and 25 times more effective than vitamin E, so it is a very powerful drink.

Green tea is also helpful in preventing cancers in other parts of the body such as the stomach, colon, ovaries, lungs, bladder, skin and particularly the prostate. It is especially important in fighting breast cancer. In fact, one oncologist in the UK has developed an anti-cancer pill, which contains concentrated green tea along with other concentrates such as turmeric, pomegranate and broccoli.

How does it work?

Green tea works in a number of different ways to protect us. It contains hundreds of powerful plant chemicals called catechins: one of the most useful is epigallocatechin gallate or EGCG. In our liver we have special enzymes that help detoxify dangerous chemicals and cancer-causing substances. Green tea enhances these, and the high level of antioxidants in it prevents fats from going rancid. Rancid fats are very toxic so this is extremely important.

Green tea can also reduce inflammation and stop cancer from spreading once it has developed. The ability of green tea to do this is no mean feat. This is because, for a tumour to spread to other sites, it has to break through the extracellular matrix or strong protective shield, which holds cells together.

Starve cancer cells

Another way that green tea can protect our breasts is by stopping tiny tumours or clusters of cells establishing the network of blood vessels they need to survive. In order to grow, they need oxygen and nutrients like any other living thing. These are carried in the blood via blood vessels so they have to grow new ones. This is called 'angiogenesis'. If the small tumours cannot get a blood supply, they starve to death.

However, before these blood vessels start to grow on a tumour, they need a signal. As mentioned earlier, this signal is called vascular endothelial growth factor (VEGF). Chemicals in green tea can lower this.

Green tea can also lower oestrogen. For those with hormone-dependent breast cancer, oestrogen is important because, as you know, some breast cancers grow with oestrogen. In post-menopausal women, oestrogen is made from male hormones in the body. The enzyme aromatase can stop this. Studies in test tubes have found that the polyphenols in green tea are able to inhibit this enzyme. Because of this it used to be thought that green was of benefit to pre-menopausal women only. However, later research has shown that it can also help post-menopausal women reduce their risk as well.

Killing themselves

Green tea also has many other attributes. One is that it can make cancer cells self-destruct. This is called 'apoptosis' or cell suicide and is the way that our bodies deal with damaged cells. About a million cells are replaced every second in this way. The problem with cancer cells is that they can resist apoptosis and keep on growing regardless. It is amazing, therefore, that the chemicals in green tea can help the body work as it should.

As well as helping prevent breast cancer, green tea can lower cholesterol and blood pressure and help prevent urinary tract infections. It also has a calming effect on the body, as it stimulates alpha waves in the brain. These induce both relaxation and better concentration at the same time. Quite a powerful substance!

How to use green tea

It should be brewed for more than just a few minutes. If brewed for five minutes only 20 per cent of the catechins are extracted but if you brew it for eight to 10 minutes you get much more.

It is better to buy organic green tea as some non-organic varieties have been found to contain DDT, an oestrogenic pesticide. Most supermarkets now stock various delicious green teas, some with lemon and other interesting flavours. Make sure, however, that any flavouring added is natural and not some manufactured chemical.

For those who really do not like this drink, or could not get to like it, supplements and capsules are available but I always feel it is better to ingest the real thing where you can.

Synergy again

Why not enhance the health-giving properties of your green tea by taking it with a meal including turmeric or a sandwich filled with fresh organic salad. Studies have shown that consuming green tea with turmeric can substantially enhance both substances. However, I don't expect you to put turmeric directly in your tea, although that is possible! In the chapter on fruit we saw that lemons enhance the properties of green tea so why not try green tea with real organic lemon?

Water

We are all two-thirds water. Good water is vital for health. We cannot exist for longer than four days without it. Not drinking enough water can make us dehydrated and cause such problems as constipation, fatigue, dry skin, mouth and lips, joint problems, dark urine, headaches, dizziness and lack of concentration. We need about six to eight glasses of water a day, more on a hot day, or if you are exercising and sweating a lot.

It is difficult to know what to say about water because information on local water is not very easy to get. However, some argue that it is full of hormone-disrupting chemicals. Many people are now buying bottled water and sales have escalated in the last few years. I am not sure whether that is because they believe that tap water is polluted or because they like the taste of bottled water better.

The quality of bottled water is variable and some is no better than tap water. However, it is best to buy natural mineral water from a reputable company. Water from plastic bottles is not good because chemicals from the plastic can leach into the water, especially if it is left in the sun and heat. Good water in glass bottles is an option but be careful to buy it from a reputable company.

Tap water

Tap water is not really the fresh natural water that we would have drunk in earlier times, as it has been recycled and then treated, and can contain chlorine and fluoride, as well as nitrates and agricultural chemicals. It is not known whether it contains hormones but there has been speculation that it does, and some argue that it is full of them. I do not know exactly what your water is like. However, I recommend filtering it in some way with either a charcoal filter or a more sophisticated system like reverse osmosis. Reverse osmosis is often thought to be the best way to get clean water, although one of the parts is apparently made from plastic which might leach oestrogen into the water. It can be expensive too and it does take minerals from the water. This can be mitigated by all the vegetables and fruit that I am hoping you will eat. In any event, I do recommend that you try to drink good water which is as uncontaminated as possible. Drinking fresh vegetable juices is one way to reduce the amount of water you have to drink but you still need water.

Other drinks

Coffee can be dehydrating. Fizzy drinks, cordials and squashes are not good because they usually contain sugar and artificial additives. Fresh fruit juices should always be diluted.

CHAPTER 13

Just what your cells need

What about fish? You have probably heard how good it is for your heart. You might also have given it to your children to help their brain development. However, did you know that it can also affect breast cancer?

Eating the right fats really can affect your health dramatically. However, of all the foods described in this book, the most confusion exists about fats and oils. Fats have had a very bad press and often you get the impression that all fats are bad, make you fat and cause heart disease. This is not the case. The truth is that some fats are so important to health that they are called 'essential fatty acids'. This is because our bodies cannot make them, so they must be obtained through our diet. Eating the right fats and not eating the wrong ones can dramatically affect your chances of having heart disease, cancer and a host of other diseases and conditions.

The problem is that over time we have replaced the fats that we are supposed to eat with new and changed fats that are not found in nature. This is perhaps the biggest change in our diet since time began. These new fats can cause untold damage. We will look at these in chapter 24.

This chapter, however, will show how certain fats and oils can lower your chances of getting breast cancer in the first place, and help prevent it returning if you have been a victim.

The right fat

Fish that swim in cold waters need to contain oil that stays liquid in that chilly environment. Imagine if their bodies were full of butter or a fat that is solid at room temperature. Their muscles would go hard and they would not be able to move properly. The fat in cold water fish is in fact liquid at room temperature and does not turn solid until the temperature reaches -103 degrees Fahrenheit. It is called omega-3 and has been found to have a dramatic effect on the prevention of all sorts of diseases. The fish we are talking about here are salmon, sardines, trout, mackerel, herring and anchovies.

Why are these so important for both our brains and our bodies? The reason is that our bodies are made from cells and these cells have a membrane surrounding them. This protects the cell in that it controls what goes in and what goes out. In humans, it is made from fats or phospholipids, which just means fats and phosphorus, but it needs the right fats in order to function properly. These are omega-3 from fish oil and omega-6 from nuts and seeds.

The problem is that whatever fats you eat will become part of that membrane. If you eat the wrong fats, the body will do its best and use these instead but they will not work as well or protect the cell as well.

We are not eating fish as much as we used to and the oils we are eating are the processed, manufactured oils that you see everywhere in the supermarket. If we do not eat enough fish oil, our cell membranes will be made from any of the unhealthy oils that we do eat, will become harder and more rigid and have more difficulty protecting us. Your body will take what you give it. So give it what it really needs. Give it oily fish.

Omega-3 deficiencies are common

Intake of fish has decreased dramatically during the last 100 years. People in different countries all over the world have different levels of omega-3 in their cells. In countries like Sweden, fish could have been eaten seven days a week. In fact, at one time it was so common for Swedish workers to be given fish every day for lunch that employees had it written into their contracts that they were not to be given it more than a few times a week.

It is not just the amount of omega-3 that matters but also the ratio of omega-3 to omega-6. People in Europe and America have high levels of omega-6 and low levels of omega-3. There is far too much omega-6 in the modern diet compared to omega-3. The Japanese have the opposite and so do Eskimos. How do you tell if you might be deficient in omega-3? One symptom is dry skin. You could have a dry, scaly rash, dry eyes, cracked nails, poor wound healing and rough, bumpy skin on the outside of your upper arms.

Fish oil and breast cancer

What has all this to do with breast cancer? What evidence is there that fish is so protective to your breasts? Well, studies all over the world have shown that those who eat the most fish have the least breast cancer. This is an observation, so does not prove a causal relationship, but other types of studies back this up. Omega-3 fats contain two types of fat, DHA and EPA. One recent study on mice found that DHA in fish oil could prevent breast cancer cells from metastasising to the bones. It also found that DHA can strongly cause human breast cancer cells to self-destruct (apoptosis) in a diet supplemented with 5 per cent fish oil. It also stopped the cancer cells proliferating. Another study on mice in the *Journal of Nutritional Biochemistry* stated that, 'we provide, for the first time, unequivocal evidence that omega-3 is causally linked to tumour prevention'.

One very important review in *The British Medical Journal* (The BMJ) looked at the relationship between oily fish and breast cancer. They looked at 26 different publications that included 20,905 cases of breast cancer and 883, 585 controls (people who did not have breast cancer). The authors found that marine omega-3 was associated with a 14 per cent reduction in risk and stated, 'the risk of getting breast cancer was reduced by 5 per cent per day per 0.1g of EPA+DHA a day'. They made the point that this equates with one to two portions a week.

Easy and different ways to use oily fish

- While fresh fish is better, you can sometimes use tinned sardines (in water) in salads and sandwiches.

- Chop fresh, organic salmon and add to your pizza dishes.

- Mix oily fish with rice for an interesting risotto.

- Add chopped fish to pizzas and include with vegetables.

- Try pickled herring, chopped herring (without added oil) or herring rollmops. These are stocked by most supermarkets.

Farmed salmon

It is better to eat wild salmon if you can get it. Farmed salmon may not contain the right balance of essential fatty acids if the fish haven't been fed correctly. Often they are given cereals rather than the plankton (small fish) that they are supposed to eat. This means that, since the omega-3 comes from these little fish, the salmon themselves will be low in these essential fats. In addition, when serving salmon it is better not to add mayonnaise as the good oils in the fish will then have to compete with the very inferior oil in the dressing.

What if you really hate oily fish?

If this is the case, you can still get your omega-3s by eating flaxseeds and walnuts. However, these are not the same as fish. This is because the oil in these has to be converted to the DHA and EPA found naturally in fish oil. Many adults are not good at making this conversion.

You can take fish oil capsules instead. However, if you are going to do this, you need to make sure that you get them from a reputable source. In particular, the oil has to be free of contaminants from the sea so it has to have been cleaned up. This may be made clear on the label. Otherwise, you will need to ask in the shop or contact the manufacturer. It also has to be taken within the sell-by date, kept fresh and not left in heat or light.

Be careful not to make the mistake of buying cod liver oil capsules in order to increase your levels of omega-3. Cod liver oil was given to children after the war to prevent rickets or bent bones and is a very good source of vitamins A and D. However, it is not a good source of fish oil as cod is not an oily fish. Also, because it is so high in vitamins A and D, it is easy to overdose on it. What you need to buy is something that just says omega-3 fish oil or salmon oil.

Because of the fact that there is pollution in the sea, and fish can be affected by this, some nutritionists are concerned about advising people to eat fish at all. The problem is that we do need omega-3 in our diet and vegetarian sources like flaxseeds and walnuts are not exactly the same. Try to get organic or wild Alaskan salmon. Salmon farmed in the UK is not always a good option. It depends on what the farmers feed the fish. Small fish tend to be less polluted than large fish. This is because the big fish eat the smaller fish and so on. This means that big fish such as tuna tend to concentrate the toxins from the smaller fish.

Tuna packed in oil is not a good source of omega-3 fats because of the addition of processed oils. It can also be high in mercury and should not be eaten by pregnant women.

CHAPTER 14

Other essential fats and oils

Flaxseeds: a wonder food for breasts

Although the last chapter was on fats and oils, flaxseeds need a special mention. They seem to be truly remarkable in what they can do to prevent breast cancer. Surgeon Dr Christine Horner has stated that flaxseeds have more potent medicinal qualities for breast cancer than any other known edible plant. There are three main reasons why these little seeds are so protective of our breasts: they contain omega-3 fatty acids, they contain lignans and they can reduce oestrogen.

Omega-3 fatty acids

It is very important for women who are vegetarians or vegans to have another source of omega-3 fatty acids, as, apart from walnuts, there are not many foods other than fish that are high in this nutrient. However, as we have seen in the previous chapter, eating these is not the same as eating fish because, while fish oil contains EPA and DHA, the oil in flaxseeds needs to be converted to these in the body and not everyone can make this conversion easily. Yet we can see how important these omega-3 fats are for cancer prevention. They are called 'essential fatty acids' as they cannot be made in the body and need to be ingested through our diet.

Lignans

Flaxseeds also contain lignans. These are compounds that give plants their hard structure and enable them to stay upright and not flop about. Lignans are found in other foods such as broccoli, carrots and asparagus but they are extremely high in flaxseeds. Apparently, flaxseeds contain 100 times more lignans than any other plant.

Lignans can help prevent breast cancer in many ways. One study found that flaxseeds reduced the growth of human ER-negative breast cancer in mice and prevented it travelling to other parts of the body. The mice were fed their normal diet or the normal diet plus flaxseed. Metastasis to their lymph nodes was reduced by 52 per cent in the group getting flaxseed oil compared to those eating their normal diet and metastasis to their lungs was reduced by 16 to 70 per cent.

Another study in the journal *Cancer Causes & Control* found that eating flaxseeds was associated with a significant reduction in breast cancer in women who consumed them at least once a week.

Reducing oestrogen

Another way in which flaxseeds can help prevent breast cancer is by reducing levels of oestrogen in your body. As we have already seen in relation to green tea, male hormones in your body (androgens) can be converted to oestrogen using an enzyme called aromatase. Anything that stops or inhibits this happening is a good thing. Lignans in flaxseeds are another example of food chemicals that can block the actions of this enzyme.

Lignans can also prevent cancerous cells getting the blood supply they need to grow as they can block the chemical VEGF (see page 55).

Flaxseeds are also high in fibre. You can see this if you put them in a glass with water as a soft jelly-like substance is formed. This is very soothing to the intestines and that is why flaxseeds are good for constipation. For breast cancer prevention, fibre binds to oestrogen and helps take it out of the body. Incidentally, fibre takes excess cholesterol out of the body in the same way, so flaxseeds can help with this too.

How can you use flaxseeds?

Having said all that, you might feel that you want to begin eating flaxseeds as soon as possible. However, how can you use them? You can add them to cereals, cooked brown rice or salads, or just eat them on their own from a spoon. They should be ground as they are quite hard and fibrous and might not be absorbed properly otherwise. It is better to grind them yourself, as the shells are there to keep them fresh. You can use a coffee grinder for this. It is better to grind just a small amount at a time and keep them in a sealed container in the fridge. Buy organic if you can.

If you do not like eating flaxseeds, you can use flaxseed oil, although it will lack the fibre and some of the co-factors that are included in the whole seed. However, you should not cook with flaxseed oil, as the heat will oxidise it and this is not something you want in your body. If you buy flaxseed oil, it must be kept very fresh in a dark bottle in the fridge and used within a short period. Even the shop where you buy it from must keep it in the fridge. The oil can be used as a salad dressing, a bread dip instead of butter or mixed with yogurt or cottage cheese.

If you really do not like the taste of these seeds or the oil, capsules are available. These too should be refrigerated.

How much should you take? Dr Michael Murray recommends one tablespoon of organic flaxseed oil a day or one or two tablespoons a day of ground flaxseeds.

Walnuts

Walnuts are a great food. They are quick and easy to prepare, need no cooking, are completely natural and are full of vitamins, minerals and cancer-fighting compounds. They are a wonderful addition to your diet. They can protect us in all sorts of ways but for those who fear breast cancer they are a great boon. This is because they contain the essential fatty acids that we discussed earlier, particularly omega-3.

In a very recent study, mice were given the equivalent of two ounces of walnuts a day and then had breast cancer cells grafted onto them. Researchers compared those not given walnuts with those given the same diet but with the addition of walnuts. The mice receiving the walnuts had a reduced incidence of breast cancer and fewer and smaller tumours when they did get it. The researchers made the point that the omega-3 was not the only thing that was having this effect. There appeared to be other chemicals in walnuts that were also protective.

For men, walnuts are a blessing because they may also have the power to help prevent prostate cancer. Another very recent study on cancers grafted onto mice found that of those who had been given walnuts, only 18 per cent developed prostate tumours. However, of those that were not given walnuts, 44 per cent succumbed and their tumours were much larger.

Be careful, however, if you eat lots of nuts and seeds and no fish, especially if you also eat any foods with added oils. You could become deficient in omega-3 as seeds contain quite a high proportion of omega-6.

Keep them fresh

Like all nuts, walnuts have to be kept very fresh because rancid oil can affect our health. Ideally, it would be better to buy them in shells and crack them yourself. After all, the shell is there to protect the nut and keep it fresh. Rancid oil is something you do not want in your body. However, it is not always easy to find nuts in shells. They tend to be around only during the Christmas period. If you do buy them shelled, keep them in an airtight container in the fridge and do not let them go beyond the sell-by date. Although walnuts can be expensive, buying walnut pieces or ones sold for cooking make it more economical.

Walnuts are a great snack to eat between meals. For meals, they can be added to salads such as Waldorf salad, which contains only diced apple, chopped celery and walnuts with a nice dressing. They can also be added to your morning cereal if you eat one. Make sure you chew them well to make them easier to digest. If you really cannot digest them well, you can always grind them with a coffee grinder and sprinkle them on other food such as brown rice. It is better not to bake with ground nuts as the heat can cause oxidation, and to eat them fresh to preserve the nutrients, especially the essential fatty acids.

Brazil nuts

Brazil nuts are high in the mineral selenium. We need to get enough selenium in our diet because low levels have been linked to greater risk of nearly all cancers, including breast cancer. Getting enough selenium is important because it increases levels of the liver enzyme, glutathione peroxidase. This is an antioxidant which changes dangerous hydrogen peroxide to water.

Apparently, 200 mcg of selenium a day has been associated with a 50 per cent lower risk of breast cancer. To get this amount, eat a few organically grown Brazil nuts every day. This is easy and pleasant to do but packs a punch for the prevention of breast cancer. Selenium is also found in other foods such as onions, leafy greens and mushrooms, but Brazil nuts have the most. The human body needs just a small amount of selenium and high doses can be toxic, so do not overdo it.

Olive oil

This type of oil has become very popular in recent years. It is not an essential oil like omegas-3 and 6 but it is still quite healthy. It contains omega-9 among other fatty acids. It is now used in salads and dressings, and supermarkets are full of varieties from all over Europe. There are different types of olive oil, depending on how the extraction was carried out, but extra virgin olive oil is the one that is nearest to the oil in its natural state. One study carried out in the Spanish island of Gran Canaria found that those eating the most olive oil had the lowest risk of breast cancer. Another very recent study found that in an experimental model, diets high in omega-6 fats stimulated breast cancer cells whilst those containing extra virgin olive oil did not.

If you cook with olive oil, you should not allow it to smoke. In fact, it is better not to use it for cooking at all but instead to have it in salads as they do in the Mediterranean. They also dip their pitta bread in it rather than using butter.

It is also important to choose a good quality olive oil. Some have been processed to a degree and are not much better than the processed oils that we will look at in more detail in chapter 24. You need an organic extra virgin olive oil but be careful where it comes from.

Olive oil, like any other fat, is high in calories so will contribute to weight gain if used in large quantities.

CHAPTER 15

Fabulous fibre

What is fibre?

Fibre is the part of the plant that we do not really absorb. Because of this, it used to be thought that it was unimportant and could be left out of the human diet. It was later discovered that even though it was not absorbed it had many functions to perform in the body. Without enough fibre, we can become constipated. This makes us more likely to succumb to all the complaints of a low fibre diet, which can lead to a variety of illnesses, such as irritable bowel syndrome and even bowel cancer. Fibre used to be called 'roughage' but this is a misnomer because it really is not rough at all and helps the smooth passage of faecal matter through the body, making the stool less dense, softer and bulkier. Fibre works by attracting water like blotting paper. The added water keeps everything soft. Fibre can be divided into soluble and insoluble. Soluble fibre forms a jelly-like substance when mixed with water. It is made up of gums and pectins found in fruit and vegetables, is also present in oats and is very high in flaxseeds. This type lowers cholesterol and helps constipation. Insoluble fibre is good for making the stool more bulky. It is found in whole wheat, wheat bran and root vegetables like carrots and swede.

Meat, eggs, white bread, cheese and sweets contain no fibre at all so eating too much of these can be very constipating and acid-forming.

Fibre and breast cancer

A diet containing enough fibre is important for the prevention of breast cancer. One way that fibre can protect the breasts is by removing excess oestrogen from the body. The oestrogen attaches itself to the fibre and is excreted via the stool. It also prevents oestrogen from being reabsorbed into the body.

A very recent study compared the diets of 382 Malaysian women with breast cancer and 382 women who were similar in many ways but who did not have breast cancer. It showed that pre-menopausal and post-menopausal women who ate the most fibre were 70 per cent less likely to develop cancer than those eating the least. Although this was just a single study a systematic review of 16 prospective cohort studies published in *Annals of Oncology* came up with similar results.

However, one case-control study found that only fruit and vegetable fibre decreased the risk of breast cancer. It found that there was a 52 per cent risk reduction for a high intake of vegetable fibre and a 46 per cent risk reduction for a high intake of fruit fibre. Strangely enough, there was no association between eating fibre from grains and the risk of breast cancer. This may be because it was not just the fibre itself that caused the decrease but the other properties of the fruit and vegetables. We can see, therefore, that fruit and vegetables have many different anti-cancer protective properties which operate simultaneously.

Fibre also removes excess cholesterol in the same way as it removes oestrogen so this gives us an added benefit.

As in everything you can also have too much fibre. It is not good to give children bran cereals as these can take nutrients out of the body.

How to include more fibre in your diet

If you increase fibre in your diet, you need to increase water as fibre binds to the water.

- Eat lots of vegetables and some fruit. Try to eat lightly cooked ones, as much of the fibre is destroyed by cooking.

- Eat porridge oats, brown rice, millet and quinoa. A truly natural cereal like porridge oats is far better than processed boxed cereals sold in the supermarket.

- Eat flaxseeds which are high in fibre and very good for constipation. Drink lots of water with them.

- Eat dried prunes and figs which are high in fibre and good if you crave something sweet.

- Eat peas, beans, lentils, nuts and seeds which are all good sources of fibre.

- It is not a good idea to eat lots of bran for fibre.

CHAPTER 16

Spice up your life

The modern British diet seems to have become spicier in the last few years and that is certainly a good thing. Many spices contain anti-cancer properties that have just become known in recent years. They actually contain more antioxidants than any other food. Dr Richard Béliveau, a scientific researcher on antioxidants, has stated that at one time cinnamon was so prized that it was considered more precious than gold. He has also said that it has one of the highest antioxidant contents of the entire vegetable world. Although blueberries are very high in cancer-protecting polyphenols and proanthocyanidins, weight for weight cinnamon is 25 times higher. Of course, it is true that we would not choose to eat large quantities of this spice but it is a good idea to eat some of it regularly.

Ginger

This interesting spice contains the chemical gingerol, which has been shown to have anti-cancer properties. In fact, scientists in Japan have found 14 chemicals in ginger that are stronger antioxidants than vitamin E. Because of this, it was sometimes used as a preservative and it has been used as a medicine for literally thousands of years. It has antioxidant and anti-inflammatory properties and can even reduce the nausea from chemotherapy.

You can use it as a tea by boiling some fresh ginger in water and adding lemon. Crystallised ginger can also be eaten occasionally. I try to rub off some of the sugar. It can also be grated in other dishes such as stews and even yogurt. There is also chocolate-coated ginger!

Cinnamon

This is a great tasting spice. It always reminds me of my childhood. When growing up in Scotland we used to buy a sweet the size of a small potato and covered in cinnamon. It is still sold there today. Cinnamon is an ancient spice – one of the oldest and most popular. It is even mentioned in the Bible. Fortunately for us, recent research has shown that it also has anti-cancer properties.

As we've seen before, in order for a tumour to grow and take hold, it needs to establish a blood supply (angiogenesis). This allows oxygen and nutrients to get to the tumour and make it grow. One study found that a water-based extract of cinnamon could stop this happening. The study concluded that cinnamon could 'potentially be useful in cancer prevention or treatment'.

This is a very versatile spice, which tastes wonderful in anything containing cooked apples. It can also be used in savoury dishes. Middle Eastern cookery uses this aromatic spice in lots of meat, rice, soup and stew dishes and it even works very well in bolognese sauce. Beef or lamb tagine is a good choice or try the wonderful spicy Moroccan tomato, chickpea and lentil soup, harira. This contains all three of the most protective anti-cancer spices – cinnamon, ginger and turmeric.

Cloves

Cloves have also been found to have anti-cancer properties. The main oil in cloves is called eugenol and a study cited in the journal *BMC Cancer* found that this oil has specific toxicity to breast cancer cells. In test tubes it made the cancer cells self-destruct (apoptosis). It also killed cancer cells that were grafted on to mice.

Cloves are another spice that go very well with anything made from apples. Cinnamon and cloves can be used together. A very easy way is to simply bake apples and use these two spices to add interest and flavour.

Fenugreek

Fenugreek seeds are not something that we immediately think of when choosing what to eat. However, research has shown that they do have anti-cancer properties. Traditionally they were used to treat high cholesterol, inflammation and digestive problems. Strangely enough, fenugreek is also recommended for increasing milk production in nursing mothers. In one in vitro study, it was found that it caused breast cancer cells to self-destruct (apoptosis). Fenugreek seeds have a very pleasant curry flavour and they can be sprouted and added to salads.

Soak the seeds overnight. The next day drain the water. Wet a clean cloth and squeeze out any excess water. Put the soaked seeds in the cloth. Tighten the cloth and put it into a covered container for one or two days. You can eat the sprouts after two days. They will stay fresh in the fridge for two to five days.

Turmeric

Of all the foods in this book, turmeric is one of the most amazing. It has so many anti-cancer functions that it is stunning. One cancer centre said that its anti-cancer effects were 'staggering'. It contains more than 24 of these compounds, including six different COX-2 inhibitors. The Latin name for turmeric is 'Curcuma longa' because one of the most important active ingredients in it is a polyphenol called curcumin. This is really something to get excited about. However, be careful not to confuse it with cumin, which is a different plant.

Turmeric is a member of the ginger family and its vivid yellow/orange hue is what gives the colour to curries. It has been used in Asian cooking for thousands of years and is beneficial for all sorts of conditions, not just cancer.

What it does

One way that turmeric helps prevent breast cancer is through the COX-2 enzyme mentioned previously. As we have already seen, the COX-2 enzyme promotes inflammation and affects cancer in various different ways. It is a wonderful thing that a natural substance like turmeric can do so much to stop the actions of this potentially dangerous enzyme. In fact, amazingly, turmeric is one of the most potent natural anti-inflammatory substances discovered and people who want to prevent cancer should eat it regularly.

Helping the liver

Dangerous chemicals have to be detoxified in the liver. Certain toxins such as those in the pesticides DDT and chlordane are particularly dangerous and can act like oestrogen in the body. Turmeric can stop the negative effects of these.

Incidentally, there is an interesting story that shows how harmful DDT can be. At one time in Israel there was a very high rate of breast cancer and it was found that farmers were using DDT and two other chemicals as a disinfectant in cow sheds. This was apparently going into the milk. When this was discovered, and they stopped using DDT, the incidence of breast cancer dropped dramatically.

Another way that turmeric protects us is by making the receptors on the breast less sensitive to oestrogen. Normally when oestrogen attaches itself to receptors on breast cells, they start to divide. Turmeric makes this happen more slowly.

Turmeric also plays a role in the prevention of heart problems by lowering levels of cholesterol in the body.

How to use turmeric

It is a good idea to have some turmeric every day, especially if you have already had breast cancer. However, it can be difficult to absorb and should be combined with black pepper and some fat. The fat could be extra virgin olive oil or coconut oil.

- Add to soups and stews that contain some fat.

- Make your own curry powder. Combine turmeric with coriander, cardamom, fenugreek and pepper.

- Add to scrambled eggs or omelettes.

- Add to any root vegetables such as potatoes, carrots or swede.

- Mix with organic brown rice for a pleasant exotic flavour.

- Have some green tea with your meal containing turmeric as having both together enhances the effects of each other.

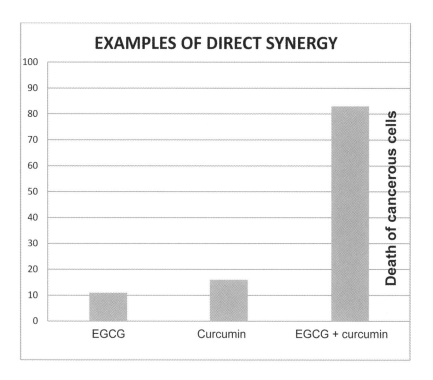

CHAPTER 17
Vegetarian diets

Some people believe that to prevent cancer we should not eat meat at all as it often contains steroids, hormones and other chemicals. I agree that we do not want these substances in our food. However, studies carried out on meat and its relationship to cancer do not usually distinguish between different kinds of meat. For example, processed meats like sausages, salami, bacon, spam and processed cooked chicken slices are very different from grass-fed organic fresh meat. I certainly think that you should not eat any processed meat at all.

Also vegetarian diets are not always healthy diets. I am sometimes asked if they are and I always answer that it all depends on what the vegetarian eats. If we define a vegetarian as someone who does not eat meat or fish, then you can still be a vegetarian and live on pizza, pasta and doughnuts. In fact, I have met a vegetarian who did just that. A meat eater who eats a little organic meat and loads of vegetables will have a healthier diet than a vegetarian who eats poor quality vegetarian foods like Quorn or fills up with pasta and cheese.

The idea is to eat the best vegetarian diet if you are a vegetarian and the best-mixed diet if you are not a vegetarian. Either way, we do need to eat many more vegetables than we have probably been used to in order to get all the cancer-protective properties that they can give us.

What might a vegetarian diet lack?

Vegetarians might be lacking some nutrients if they do not think about what they are eating or don't make sure that their diet is balanced. The main nutrients that might be lacking in a vegetarian diet are protein, zinc, iron, omega-3 fatty acids and vitamin B12.

If a vegetarian eats fish then it is easy to get enough protein that way.

However, if he or she does not eat fish, it is not always easy to find good sources of protein. Eggs are good but I do not recommend eating large amounts of cheese and protein substitutes such as Quorn. Cheese is high in fat and Quorn is a highly processed food.

Protein is made up of amino acids; a complete protein such as meat, eggs or fish contains all 22 amino acids. Vegetarian proteins such as lentils or nuts do not contain all 22 so are considered incomplete. Different protein foods contain different amino acids so you need to eat them together. Mixing foods such as beans, peas, lentils and yogurt has been the way that vegetarians traditionally made sure that they consumed all 22 and it is still important for them to do that today.

A pleasant vegetarian food that contains all 22 amino acids is quinoa. It is a little like couscous in texture and has a pleasant nutty taste. Another food that is high in protein is whey, which can be bought in health food shops.

Your heritage

If your ancestors have been vegetarian for centuries and this is their traditional diet, they would have developed the best way to use foods. Changing to a Western-style vegetarian diet full of pasta and pizzas is not a good idea, as traditional peoples have learned over hundreds of years how to combine different foods to get all their amino acids.

There is a school of thought that says that we should keep to the diet of our ancestors if we know what that was. Therefore, the Swedes who traditionally ate a large amount of fish should still be eating fish, as they are biologically adapted to it. Similarly, those who come to the UK from countries where the traditional diet is vegetarian should eat that. This is because it is the diet that sustained their ancestors over many years, and it contains what they need. The problem is that younger people of all cultures are eating more processed and wheat-based foods so they are not getting the nutrients that they used to get from their traditional diet.

Tips for healthy eating for vegetarians

- Eating enough protein is important so have complete protein regularly. Protein sources are nuts, seeds, lentils, chickpeas and beans but these need to be eaten together to get a complete protein (one which contains all of the amino acids). Whey protein can help but you need to buy a product which is of high quality.

- Combine different sorts of beans and pulses together, such as beans and lentils, rice and peas, millet and beans, especially if you're not eating fish. Eat a large variety of these different protein sources. Vegetable proteins like these need to be mixed in order to get all the amino acids.

- Vegetarians may lack omega-3 fats found in oily fish. This can cause dry skin and hair, fatigue and memory loss, and is related to breast cancer. To compensate you can eat cold pressed flax oil or flaxseeds instead, although they are not exactly the same as fish. Keep them refrigerated.

- For iron, vegetarians should consume watercress, nuts, eggs, seeds (especially pumpkin seeds), wheat germ, parsley, raisins and prunes.

- Vegetarians can get vitamin B12 from milk, yogurt and eggs but vegans should take a supplement. This is very important as B12 is contained only in animal foods.

- Vegetarians can easily become low in zinc so eat sesame seeds, walnuts, chickpeas, lentils, Brazil nuts, wholemeal bread (if no wheat allergy), beans and unsweetened popcorn. A supplement can be taken but use a multivitamin/mineral rather than individual minerals.

- Try not to eat big portions of white pasta as a filler or large amounts of cheese and dairy products. Quorn is actually a highly processed food. Use complex carbohydrates like vegetables, baked potatoes, brown rice and millet.

CHAPTER 18

Vitamin D

You may remember being given cod liver oil when you were a child. This used to be given to all children as a source of vitamin D in order to prevent bone deformities like rickets, and some still give it today. Later on, vitamin D drops were given and still are in some areas today. This is because vitamin D helps calcium to be absorbed into the bones.

Nowadays this vitamin seems to be all over the news. One doctor has said that in his entire career he has never seen a substance get the media attention that vitamin D is getting today. Reports are constantly coming in saying that people living in colder climates like the UK are not getting enough vitamin D and that this is leading to all sorts of health problems, including cancer.

Surprisingly, low levels of vitamin D is a problem that doesn't only affect people in colder climates. In fact, it is becoming evident that even people living in warmer climates are also deficient in this important vitamin.

Vitamin D comes in more than one form but the one I am referring to throughout this chapter is vitamin D3 or 25-hydroxy vitamin D (25-OH vitamin D). When we expose ourselves to the sun, vitamin D changes to become a steroid hormone. This is called vitamin D3 and this form is the one that is important for breast cancer.

What has vitamin D to do with breast cancer?

Studies have shown that those with a higher amount of vitamin D in their bodies are less likely to get breast cancer, especially if they are post-menopausal. Breast cancer is higher in areas where there is less sunlight and lower in areas where there is more. Although this in itself does not prove that low levels of vitamin D are the cause, when taken together with other studies, there is evidence that this is a major factor. The research bears this out. One study in mice showed that those with higher levels of vitamin D had only a quarter as much breast cancer as those who had not. There is now so much research on this and in fact, more than 1,000 laboratory and epidemiological studies have linked breast cancer to low levels of vitamin D.

For cancer in general, scientists have estimated that every year 60,000 premature deaths are caused by low levels of vitamin D. In a trial of 1,179 post-menopausal women in Nebraska, USA, one group of women were given calcium and vitamin D and the other group (the control group) were given a dummy pill (a placebo). It was found that those given daily calcium and vitamin D3 had a significantly lower incidence of breast cancer over four years compared with the women on the placebo. Clinical trials are seen as the gold standard of research, so here we have very good evidence of the value of vitamin D and calcium in breast cancer prevention. In 2008, a study in Canada showed that breast cancer patients with good levels of vitamin D were about half as likely to die from the disease as those patients with a serious deficiency. In addition to this, a review which looked at information from 11 case-control studies, found that the results supported 'the hypothesis that higher serum (25 OH)D) levels reduce the risk of breast cancer'.

Another very recent analysis of 30 prospective studies published in the *British Journal of Cancer* concluded, 'Our findings suggest that high vitamin D status is weakly associated with low breast cancer risk but strongly associated with better breast cancer survival'.

How does it help to prevent breast cancer?

This vitamin can help prevent breast cancer in many ways. One way is that it can stop the body producing as much oestrogen as it would without it. As you know, most breast cancers are oestrogen-positive, which means that oestrogen encourages the tumour to grow. One study found that women with the least vitamin D in their blood when diagnosed had a higher risk of the cancer returning and of dying from it.

On our breasts, we have receptors for vitamin D. That means that vitamin D can attach itself to breast cells. It is believed that this can help cancer cells die, and stop tumours getting the blood supply they need to survive. One review of 11 observational studies suggested that a blood level of '47ng/ml was associated with a 50 per cent lower risk of breast cancer.'

Sunlight and vitamin D

Vitamin D comes from the sun. It is made by the action of sunlight on the oils on our skin. However, because of the worry about the risk of skin cancer, we tend to lather ourselves with high factor sun cream when we are in the hot sun, and wear hats, sit in the shade and generally protect ourselves from its rays. Many women are also in the habit of wearing trousers in the summer as well as in the winter so this also stops the sun getting to our bodies. Daily showers and baths also remove the oil from our skins and oil is needed in order for vitamin D to be absorbed.

Even if we do not do all of the above, we are still at a disadvantage in the UK and in other Northern countries because of the small amount of sun that we actually get. If we are lucky, we get sun for just a few months of the year in the South and even less in Scotland. Billy Connolly, the Scottish comedian, says that when in the sun it takes him a week to go white, having begun as blue from the cold!

Also, in the past, we would have been outside for much of the time, hunting or foraging for food, but now we spend a lot of our time indoors. It is for these reasons therefore that very many women appear to be deficient in vitamin D when tested.

Groups likely to be deficient in vitamin D

People with darker skin produce less vitamin D from sunlight than those with lighter skin. This means that darker-skinned women need to have more exposure to sunlight. Obviously, this can be a problem for darker-skinned people living in cold climates like the UK, so they might be advised to take a supplement.

The fact that lighter-skinned women make more vitamin D from the sun is very logical and what you might expect. This is because people with lighter skins were traditionally adapted to living in colder climates with less sun. Because of this, they needed to be able to make use of any sun that was available. On the other hand, darker-skinned people who adapted to very sunny and hot climates could easily make too much vitamin D if they were in the sun for long periods, so their bodies make less to compensate. It is because of this that many studies have shown that African-Americans have very high rates of vitamin D deficiency.

Older adults

Another group who tend to make less vitamin D from the sun are older adults. As this vitamin is needed to allow the body to absorb calcium, and calcium is need for bone health, low levels of vitamin D can lead to fractures and broken bones. It has been found that as many as half of the adults with hip fractures in the USA have insufficient vitamin D.

Others who have trouble making enough vitamin D from the sun are people who are overweight. This vitamin is fat-soluble so fat cells in the body can absorb it, making it less available to other organs and tissues. This is one good reason to stay slim. Not always easy, I know.

One study of post-menopausal women in the UK found that they had low levels in their blood in the autumn when levels should be highest after the summer, and even lower levels in the spring after the winter. Women in the study who were the most overweight had the lowest levels.

How to get enough vitamin D

Very few foods contain vitamin D naturally although some have been fortified with it. Oily fish such as salmon, sardines and mackerel are among the best sources so this is another reason to eat these foods. However, even they are not particularly rich so we need to get more safe sun or take supplements.

To stay safe in the sun but to get the benefits of the vitamin D, expose some of your skin to the sun without allowing it to burn. It is better to keep away from the midday sun and to wear a hat and use sunglasses. It is possible to sit in the sun with arms and legs exposed and your face under the shade but you still need to be very careful, especially if you have pale skin, freckles or red hair. The incidence of skin cancer is still rising.

There is nothing worse than seeing fair-skinned British people at the beach lobster-red and peeling. I always worry about what they are going to feel like later that evening, having had painful bouts of sunburn myself as a child. Therefore, I am not recommending sitting in the sun at its strongest or for long. UVB radiation that produces vitamin D does not go through glass so sitting by a window does not help.

If you are going to use sunlight to get some of your vitamin D, you should not wash all the oils from your skin too quickly after being in the sun. Your body needs the oil in order to be able to make the vitamin D. This can take some hours.

I suggest that you ask your GP to test you for vitamin D3. It is a simple blood test and easy to obtain on the NHS. If it is low, take supplements and then have it retested. Remember that levels of vitamins are worked out differently in the UK from the USA so be careful if you read American sources which tell you what your levels should be.

One breast cancer surgeon said that making vitamin D free on the NHS would save 1,000 lives a year. He said that the higher the levels, the greater the protection from breast cancer.

CHAPTER 19
Beneficial bacteria/probiotics

You might wonder how bacteria can help you fight breast cancer. We have all learned that bacteria are bad and make us ill and that is true to some extent. However, not all bacteria are the same. Some do us a wonderful job in protecting our health in many ways including stopping us getting different sorts of cancer.

In our digestive tract, we have billions of bacteria called probiotics or good gut flora. Who would have thought that these microorganisms could be so valuable and important for the health of our whole system?

How probiotics protect our health

- They regulate cholesterol and maintain the immune system.

- They act like our own vitamin factory, producing the vitamins B1, B2, B3, B6, folic acid and B12 and helping in the production of other nutrients such as vitamin D. They also produce amino acids (protein) and vitamin K, needed for good bone density.

- They help the minerals calcium and iron to be absorbed.

- They do important work in our digestive system, preventing yeasts and bad bacteria taking hold.

- They attach themselves to toxic heavy metals like mercury and lead, preventing them from doing us harm.

- They stop the lining of our gut from being damaged. This is so important because if it gets damaged, substances that are not supposed to be there can get into our bloodstream.

- They protect our immune system so this helps protect us from cancer. In fact, we know that 85 per cent of our immune system is located in the digestive tract.

Breast cancer and probiotics

Beneficial bacteria or probiotics are also very important for the prevention of breast cancer because they help regulate our hormones, especially oestrogen. They can also render environmental pollutants less toxic.

In one study of cancer cells, it was found that the probiotic strains lactobacillus acidophilus and bifidobacterium infantis managed to inhibit their growth by 85 per cent after nine days. Epidemiological studies have also found that women who consumed probiotics had a lower risk of breast cancer.

In another study published in the *Journal of Clinical Immunology*, lactobacillus acidophilus taken from homemade yogurt among other things reduced tumour growth in mice. This is very good but many of us do not have the levels that we should have.

Have you lost your good bacteria?

Unfortunately, many of us have lost much of the good bacteria we might have had originally. This is because most of us have had several courses of antibiotics throughout our lives and these can kill these beneficial bacteria, as well as the bad bacteria which caused our sore throat or other infection. In addition to this, we ingest some of these antibiotics from eating meat. Antibiotics have undoubtedly been a great help to humankind, but in some cases, they have been used too much. In previous years, doctors would give probiotics every time they prescribed antibiotics. This helped to replenish some of the good bacteria that might have been killed off with the antibiotic.

Good bacteria can also be destroyed by chlorine in tap water, smoking, alcohol, stress and even flying too much. However, all is not lost. You can replace these bacteria with foods and supplements. Yogurts contain some of these but it is not easy to know how potent any particular variety is. Other foods also contain good bacteria.

Fermented foods

Many societies have fermented certain foods in order to preserve them for long periods. What they may not have known then was that this also enabled them to ingest large quantities of these wonderful beneficial bacteria. In the Middle East they have kefir, in Austria they have yogurt, while fermented vegetables like sauerkraut are eaten in Russia. In fact, very many foods can be and have been fermented. Fruits, vegetables, beans, fish, meat and soya have all been used in this way over the centuries and even today. I do not expect you to spend your life fermenting food but it might be a good idea to try to ferment a few foods such as cabbage.

Two of the main types of bacteria in fermented foods are lactobacilli and bifidobacteria. Lactobacilli are essential residents in the gut and are high in human breast milk. Bifidobacteria are more numerous. They make vitamins and assist in the absorption of calcium, iron and vitamin D.

Yogurt

This is the fermented food which is most familiar to us. Sales of yogurts have increased dramatically over the last decade but it was always a popular food in other countries. It can be made with different milks including cows', sheep's, goats' and soya, and there is now on the market an extremely delicious one made from coconut milk. If you are not going to eat dairy then I advise you to get your beneficial bacteria in some other way.

Kefir

This comes traditionally from the Caucasus mountains of Russia. In one study, kefir was able to depress the growth of breast cancer cells and showed an inhibition of proliferation of 29 per cent after six days. On the other hand, the unfermented milk extracts stimulated proliferation of the cancer cells. You can make it from kefir grains or buy it online. It is not very easy to come by in the UK. It will grow on most milks such as rice or coconut.

Fermented cabbage

This has been eaten in Russia for hundreds of years. Fermenting vegetables enabled people living in cold countries to have them throughout the whole year as they keep for many months. We now know they also contain high levels of good bacteria as described earlier. Sauerkraut is a German word that just means 'sour white cabbage'. A study published in 2013 in the *European Journal of Nutrition* found that eating cabbage and sauerkraut was associated with a reduced incidence of breast cancer. It is not difficult to make sauerkraut and once made it is delicious and can be kept for many months. Don't eat much in the beginning until you get used to the high levels of bacteria.

Kvass

This is a fermented drink often made from beetroot but sometimes from a combination of fruit and vegetables. The following recipe comes from the interesting book by Natasha Campbell-Mcbride, *Put Your Heart In Your Mouth*:

Slice a whole apple and use a teaspoon of ginger root and some berries. Put them into a litre jar. Add ½ cup of whey and top up with water. Brew for a few days at room temperature then refrigerate. Drink diluted with water.

Capsules of probiotics

All of the above foods should contain good bacteria but it might be a good idea to supplement them with capsules for a while. These contain billions of microorganisms and can be found in health food shops. You need to buy one that contains about four to ten billion of these. They need to be stored properly so read the instructions on the label; some must be refrigerated. Capsules that have a coating called 'enteric coating' are good because they stop the capsule breaking down before it reaches the colon.

If you take probiotics in capsules or more than a little fermented cabbage, you may feel off-colour to begin with as the bad bacteria die off.

CHAPTER 20
Eating for health can be fun

I know that many people have busy lives and are out all day working or juggling a job and bringing up children at the same time. If you are having treatment, you may be too tired to make elaborate meals. As a nutrition practitioner, I am keen to make food suggestions easy and practical, but sometimes people are not sure how to incorporate the different foods into their lives. Well, here are some ideas.

- Keep a bowl of cut-up vegetables, washed and ready to eat, in the fridge, to nibble on. Try carrots, broccoli, cauliflower and baby tomatoes.

- Avocados are quick and easy to prepare and are rich in nutrients. They are also good to give to young children. Cut up, they are easy for them to pick up, are soft and they seem to like them.

- Walnuts are good, but keep them in an airtight container in the fridge, as rancid oil is very bad for us.

- Make easy-peasy pea soup. Simmer frozen peas for about five minutes with some celery and mint. Blend. Onions can also be added.

- Coleslaw is easy to make. Just mix grated carrot and cabbage with a tiny bit of dressing. This is much healthier than the bad oil-laden dressings that are sold in supermarkets.

- If you love pasta, have a little but add on lots of cooked vegetables like broccoli and carrots as well as fresh salmon, and top with a decent tomato sauce. This can also be done with pizza. You get the flavour of the pizza but the advantage of all the vegetables. Keep the dough very thin.

- Soup, soup, soup made with lots of different vegetables. Soup is one of the easiest ways to ingest many cancer-protective vegetables. Have some ready for when you come in at night; it is very welcoming, especially in the winter.

- Try tinned sardines rich in omega-3 oils. It would be better to use fresh but when in a hurry, tinned can be used. Do not buy those tins that have sauces added as these usually contain processed vegetable oil. It is better to buy the ones tinned in spring water.

- Baked sweet potatoes wrapped in foil and done in the oven are very easy, and they have lower glucose-raising properties and are higher in antioxidants than ordinary potatoes.

- Try sprouting mung beans. Leave in a bowl covered with water for a few hours. Rinse every day and, in a few days, you will have a tasty salad vegetable. Children can have great fun growing them themselves.

- Bread can be difficult to digest for some people but if you love a sandwich, use thin bread and pile lots of salad vegetables inside. It's easier to eat if you make an open sandwich as they do in Sweden.

- One-pot casseroles are so easy to make. Just put it all in a pot and bake. You can choose any vegetables you like, the more the merrier, but always include garlic if you can.

- Poached organic salmon is also quick and easy to do. Just cover with water in a pot, slowly bring to the boil and simmer slowly for a few minutes until cooked.

- Nuts and different sorts of seeds are easy and protective snacks. Combined with raisins they give you a sweet taste without raising your blood sugar too high.

CHAPTER 21
Supplements

The question of supplements is controversial. Should you take them or will this just lighten your wallet with false promises for good? Health food shops are full of all kinds of different varieties, even more than shampoos at the chemist. It is not easy to know which are valuable and which are not. Some practitioners swear by them and others think that all they do is produce expensive urine.

My position on supplements is that they can be beneficial, depending on what they do and if they are used properly. However, a good diet must always come first and you cannot replace good food with pills. This is because foods contain many different phytochemicals and you cannot reproduce them all in a pill.

The nutrients in foods work together and enhance the value of each other. They are like links in a chain. For example, the fat in whole milk helps the absorption of calcium, B vitamins act with magnesium and that acts with essential oils and so on. Therefore, if you take out one vitamin or substance from a food, you are not getting the cofactors that naturally come with it. For example, we know that oranges are high in vitamin C. We can buy a supplement that just contains the vitamin itself, which is called ascorbic acid. However, if we do this, we are not getting all the other chemicals and nutrients that are found in vitamin C-rich fruit and vegetables.

In addition to this, we still do not know all there is to know about food. Nature's secrets are still being discovered. Garlic, for example, has been shown to contain about 200 different chemicals, probably more. Food is not simple. It is extremely complex.

As in the example mentioned earlier, it is better to get your vitamins from fruit and vegetables as they contain other chemicals that help the vitamins to be absorbed, along with minerals, fibre and antioxidants. A vitamin pill could never compete. However, there are times when it might be a good idea to increase your intake of some vitamins and minerals with a supplement. This might be because you have a cold and need extra, or are not in a position to eat much good food, or you need vitamin D, which is not rich in the diet.

Some supplements can help

Not all supplements are the same. Some are very simple, containing one vitamin, but some are more complex containing the whole food in a concentrated form. So, for example, a supplement of kelp, which is dried seaweed, is not the same as a supplement of vitamin B6 for these reasons. The nearer a supplement is to the real thing or the whole food the better. This means that a food concentrate in a pill such as dried whole mushroom or dried pomegranate is not the same as a pill containing a simple vitamin. Some foods are fine to take as supplements. One is garlic, which is really a food concentrate. Another is probiotics. As we saw in chapter 19, beneficial bacteria are needed in our digestive tract and many people eat yogurt in order to enhance these. However, there may not be enough probiotics in food such as yogurt to make a big difference. This is where supplements of probiotics can help.

Green drinks

We have already discussed green tea in some detail but green drinks also refer to other products such as barley grass, wheat grass, chlorella or spirulina. They are very high in nutrients, particularly chlorophyll, which is the green pigment that converts sunlight to energy. You may remember this from your biology classes at school. If you do not like these drinks, and I must admit they are not my favourite as far as taste is concerned, you can buy them in capsule form instead.

Pycnogenol

We have already seen the importance of antioxidants for cancer protection and know that vitamins C and E are potent examples found in fruit and vegetables. However, there are substances that are even more powerful than these and one of these is Pycnogenol. It is twenty times more powerful than vitamin C and fifty times more powerful than vitamin E. There is an interesting story attached to Pycnogenol. In 1535, the French explorer Jacques Cartier was stuck in the frozen St Lawrence River in Canada. On the ship he only had biscuits and frozen meat. Because there was no vitamin C available, his men would all have died of scurvy before long.

Luckily, they were rescued by the local Native Americans who showed them how to brew a tea from pine bark and needles. This contained tiny amounts of vitamin C and large amounts of a bioflavonoid. Then in the 1950s, a French professor managed to extract certain chemicals from pine bark. He called these Pycnogenol and patented them. A similar type of proanthocyanidin was taken from grape seed. These are among the most powerful antioxidants ever discovered.

Grape seed extract

Grape seed extract is also rich in proanthocyanidins and recent laboratory studies have suggested that it can play a part in the prevention of breast cancer. One study published in the *European Journal of Nutrition* found that grape seed extract in high concentrations inhibited cell proliferation and caused apoptosis (cancer cells self-destructing). The authors concluded that, 'These results make grape seed extract a powerful candidate for developing preventive agents against cancer metastasis' (cancer spreading to other organs).

Grape seed extract is also an aromatase inhibitor, which, as we have seen, can prevent male hormones in a woman's body being converted to oestrogen by way of the enzyme aromatase. In one study, where tumours were grafted on to mice, the grape seed extract was found to reduce the growth of these tumours. Grape seed extract is cheaper than Pycnogenol and, although not the same, appears to be effective.

CHAPTER 22
Unhelpful foods

Every day the media is full of information about what not to eat. We are told that we should eat this, we shouldn't eat that (often foods we like), eat more of this, cut down on that. It is a wonder there is anything left for us to eat at all. I initially decided to keep this book positive and concentrate on what we should eat. However, the information would not be complete if I did not explain why other foods are not good, especially foods that have been heavily promoted by the food industry.

You might ask why we don't just eat what we like and not think about it. Why do we have to keep wondering if things are good or bad for us? In former times, we were able to do just that. Foods were natural and unprocessed – all we had to do was eat what was around us and all we had to worry about was not getting enough food. However, now our food has changed dramatically and particularly in the last 1,000 years or so since the agricultural revolution.

In addition to this, in the last 100 years or so, we have learned how to process foods: so much so that food has become unrecognizable from what we traditionally ate. Most of us are eating very different foods from those that sustained us over the millennia and this is the cause of many of the health problems that we suffer from today.

Today some isolated cultures are still eating the traditional, unprocessed diet of their ancestors. Sadly, these groups are few and far between. However, as we saw in chapter 2, these societies do very well only if they stick to this diet. When they begin to consume Western processed food from the more industrialised countries, they start to get all the diseases that exist in these countries, particularly diabetes, heart disease and cancer.

Eating is something we do every day. It is ordinary. It does not have the glamour of high-tech laboratories and men in white coats researching into chemicals and drugs. However, do not be fooled into thinking that food cannot produce outstanding outcomes. Every cell in the body, every bone, hormone and blood cell, everything we are is made from the food we eat, even our genes.

What is wrong with our food?

On the other hand, some might argue that nobody in the West is undernourished. We have supermarkets at every street corner over-laden with every sort of tempting morsel you can think of. This is true, but a good deal of what is sold in supermarkets is full of empty calories without contributing much to our health. We know that so much of it is lacking in important nutrients like vitamins, minerals and the phytochemicals that help prevent cancers of all kinds including breast cancer.

Even worse, much of the food sold as 'healthy' is in fact the complete opposite. Therefore, often people who are trying their best to eat an excellent diet are being tempted into buying foods which are heavily marketed as healthy, but are, in fact, highly processed and often worse than many ordinary foods.

You might think that bad food would not be sold. This is not so. As far as the law is concerned, food has to be safe but not necessarily healthy. This means that it cannot contain dirt, dangerous material or bacteria, which would cause listeria or salmonella poisoning. But it doesn't have to be particularly helpful for our health or development. One joker noted that food should not kill us in the short term but it is fine if it kills us in the long term.

In addition to this, much of the food in supermarkets is designed to be tempting, tasty and almost addictive, but is not found anywhere in the natural world.

The reasons why some of our food is so bad are listed here.

- **Food processing:** Much of our food is very different from the food we used to eat. Take bread and white pasta, for example. These come from wheat, which is made up of three parts: the starch, the bran and the germ. It is the germ which contains practically all of the vitamins and minerals, but when the wheat is processed, the germ is thrown away or given to animals. The remaining starch is made into white flour and all the resulting products like bread, cereals, pasta, biscuits and cakes are made just from this devitalised portion. No wonder it does not nourish us. This is also true of other products such as white rice. Another factor is that the wheat of today is very different from the wheat of yesteryear.

- **Food storage:** Food is often stored for long periods and travels long distances before it gets to us. This causes it to lose vitamins and other nutrients.

- **Farming practices:** Because of modern farming practices, the soil on which the food is grown is not as rich in nutrients as it should be. If the nutrient is not in the soil, it cannot get into the food and therefore it cannot get into our brains. This is particularly true of minerals like magnesium, chromium, selenium, zinc and manganese.

- **Food choices and marketing:** Many people simply like unhealthy food. The problem is that marketing has encouraged people to think of some bad foods as healthy. One of the biggest cons in the food industry I would say are so-called 'health' bars, which often just contain a few vitamins and minerals added to sugar, flour and processed fat. Bars containing healthy foods like oats are often higher in sugar than chocolate.

Pasta disaster

Pasta is often seen as a very healthy food. It has had a great press because it is low in fat and quite cheap, but it is also low in vitamins, minerals and most other nutrients that you need. White pasta is almost 100 per cent starch, which will fill you up but will give you little nutrition. If you find this hard to believe, ask yourself where pasta comes from. It is wheat. What goes for white flour discussed before goes for pasta. This means that for white pasta, the bran and germ of the wheat are discarded and the pasta is made just from the starch. This has very little nutritive value except carbohydrates and empty calories. It is also lacking in most vitamins and minerals and other nutrients such as essential fats and antioxidants.

Many people appear to be living on pasta, so much so that they seem to have a craving for it. In fact, many appear to be addicted to it. Why should this be? The reason is that wheat is now grown with very high levels of gluten in order to make it springier. Gluten is a protein which is very difficult for many people to digest, and many children simply cannot cope with it. Yet people seem to crave it and want it for every meal. Craving a food is often a sign of sensitivity to that food and the worst offenders appear to be wheat, eggs, citrus and dairy products.

Wheat is everywhere

Have you noticed how many pasta/pizza restaurants have opened up recently? Have you noticed how many foods contain wheat? Examples are sandwiches, cakes, biscuits, all sorts of pasta, spaghetti, cereals, buns and bagels. There are also lots of foods with wheat and dairy combined such as pizzas, lasagne, cheese sandwiches, macaroni cheese and cheese scones. Moreover, these often also contain tomato, another food regularly implicated in food intolerance. Children in particular can become sensitive to various foods, leading to hyperactivity and problems at school.

Are these foods addictive?

Some people crave these foods so much that they eat them at every meal. They might have wheat-based cereals and toast for breakfast, sandwiches for dinner and pasta or spaghetti for their evening meal. Biscuits for morning and afternoon breaks complete the picture of a constant injection of wheat throughout the whole day.

There are three main problems with this. One is that a lot of wheat is highly processed and is low in vitamins, minerals and other important nutrients and antioxidants. Secondly, being so filling, it crowds out other more nutritious foods such as vegetables, fruit and fish.

The third reason is the most important. Some scientists argue that, because wheat is so difficult to digest, it can irritate the lining of the digestive tract, making it more permeable than it should be. This results in large proteins being able to get into the bloodstream when they should not. The body sees these as foreign and starts to react against these proteins, causing diseases where the body begins attacking itself. These diseases are called autoimmune diseases and examples are thyroiditis, colitis and rheumatoid arthritis.

Boxed cereals

Most boxed cereals are sweets. Someone once said that they are so lacking in nutrients that you might as well eat the box. Most are high in sugar, white flour and chemical additives. Often people think that eating cereal for breakfast is 'natural'. When I tell them that sometimes I have soup for breakfast, they look at me as if I am mad. However, why not? The problem is that many people have been eating cereal for breakfast every day since they were small, so it seems obvious and natural to do this. It is so common that most people do not realise that eating these wheat-based cereals for breakfast is an entirely new idea. Eating these has come about only in the last century and is completely different from what we might have eaten for most of our previous history. Some boxed cereals are of course better than others. Porridge is a complete natural grain and some brands of muesli are fine, as long as any nuts it contains are very fresh, but most of the others are just like eating sweets.

Fizzy drinks

These are high in sugar and even the low calorie ones are little more than water with lots of chemicals included – not a good idea for any of us. Some also contain phosphoric acid, which is so strong that it can strip the chalk from your shower head. It used to be a fun thing for new dental students to put a tooth in a glass of cola and find it dissolved some hours later. It is associated with lower bone density in women and can cause osteoporosis (brittle bones). Fizzy drinks that contain caffeine can make children overactive.

Fried foods

These are all high in the wrong type of fats: processed and fried poly-unsaturated oils which are particularly bad for breast cancer protection. We will look at these in more detail in chapter 24. Fried foods include chips, all types of crisps (even those made from vegetables or organic oil), battered fish and chicken, samosas, spring rolls and many snack foods. It is possible to have healthier chips, which can be made with a little olive oil and baked in the oven. Just heat olive oil in the oven, add chip-shaped potatoes and bake. However, it is not good to have these often.

'Health' bars

Please do not be fooled by these. There are many so-called 'health' bars on the market, which really contain only white flour, some grains, sugar and a few vitamins. It is best to avoid these as they are just highly processed foods not much better than chocolate bars.

The question of meat

Should we eat red meat or not? Many studies have indicated that eating red meat can increase our rate of developing breast cancer. One very large prospective cohort study called the Nurses' Health Study looked at the relationship between meat eating and breast cancer. This was a huge study, which looked at the diets of over 88,000 nurses over a period of 20 years. The nurses were asked to write down everything they ate during this time. The study showed that total intake of red meat was indeed associated with a higher incidence of breast cancer. The study also found that women who had replaced meat with legumes in early adulthood had a much lower rate.

The problem is that many of these studies do not distinguish between different types of meat. Processed meat is very different from fresh meat and organically raised meat is different from non-organically raised meat. Cows are supposed to eat grass and when we imagine them being fed, we bring to mind pictures of them roaming about the fields chewing away happily. However, the reality is very different. More often than not, they are kept in factories, given grain to eat instead of grass and then dosed with antibiotics and steroids. This produces a very different kind of meat from the meat our ancestors thrived on. I suggest that if you do eat some meat, eat only grass-fed organic beef and do not have it often. It is better to use it to add flavour to your plate of vegetables or in a large stew where it is not the main ingredient. There are some, however, who say that meat in general is not good because the saturated fat in it can promote inflammation.

Processed meat

Processed meats like luncheon meats, hot dogs, bologna, spam, most sausages, salami, ham, hot dogs, corned beef and pre-packed turkey slices have added problems. They are often thinly sliced and sold in vacuum wrapped packaging. They are not good because they are highly salted, full of artificial additives and often preserved with nitrites. A very recent study in the *International Journal of Epidemiology* found that processed meat was associated with a higher risk of breast cancer. However, this study was particularly interesting because when one group was given antioxidants with the meat, the cancer-causing effect was stopped. This suggests that the antioxidants protected them from developing cancer.

However, I still say that you should keep away from processed meats. They do not add anything to our lives and are not very difficult to give up. If you do eat some meat, it is best to buy fresh organic meat, cook it yourself and just have it occasionally.

In 2007 the World Cancer Research Fund and the American Institute for Cancer Research reviewed more than 7,000 clinical studies and concluded that no amount of processed meat is safe and no one should eat it.

Salt

Modern processed food is loaded with salt. Salt is really sodium chloride and the levels of sodium and potassium in our bodies should be balanced. Potassium comes from fresh fruit and vegetables and is high in natural, unprocessed food. Before the advent of food processing we ate very little salt and very many more fruit and vegetables than we do today. This gave us high levels of potassium and low levels of sodium. Today this ratio has been reversed. Now we eat so many foods which are full of salt, such as crisps, chips, peanuts, smoked fish, bought soups and so on. It is obvious that these foods contain so much salt as they taste salty. Even if we buy a salad in a restaurant, some of the foods included such as dressings, olives, and anything tinned such as sweetcorn will be high in added salt.

Salt is everywhere

There are many other foods which, although they contain quite high levels of salt, do not taste particularly salty. For example, you probably would not think that bread contained salt if you had not read the label. Other foods like breakfast cereals, ready meals and savoury snacks also contain high levels of salt. Pizzas contain high levels of salt, both from the crust and from the cheese. Processed meats like salami are very high in salt. Even cornflakes contain salt. Therefore, you can see that throughout the day, if we eat supermarket-packaged food, we are ingesting a huge amount of salt.

If you are going to eat salty food, you could try to balance the sodium by eating some fruit or drinking some fruit juice in order to increase the level of potassium. Human milk contains three times as much potassium as sodium, which gives us an indication of what the ratio should be.

Excess salt drives cancer. One Israeli study of 326 breast cancer cases and 415 disease-free controls found that those on a low salt diet had significantly less breast cancer than those on a diet containing a lot of salt. Incidentally, the same study found that those working in textile, clothing and other industries had a higher rate than those doing administrative work.

Dairy products

In the West, we have been taught to believe that dairy products are very good for us. Some of you will remember the old advert 'Drinka Pinta Milka Day'. Children were given it free at school and one confectionary company advertised its product as containing a pint of milk. However, the geochemist Dr Jane Plant has argued that milk is not good for us at all. She makes the point that humans are the only species that will drink the milk of another animal. When you think about it, it is obvious that milk is meant as a food for young cows, goats or sheep.

Dr Plant argues that milk contains a significant amount of 'insulin-like growth factor 1' (IGF-1). This has been shown to promote the growth of breast cancer cells in test tubes. In addition to this, it appears that pre-menopausal women with high levels of IGF-1 have a higher risk of breast cancer. Dr Christine Horner argues that the protein in milk known as casein stops IGF-1 from breaking down. It is also true that women in China, who do not consume dairy, have very little incidence of breast cancer compared to those in the West. She argues that this is because cow's milk contains over 35 different hormones and 11 growth factors, including oestrogen. In fact, she makes a very good, detailed and convincing case for not drinking milk from any animal (cow, goat or sheep) or consuming any products made from it.

In relation to this, one study published by the National Cancer Institute found that those who consume more high fat dairy products have a greater risk of breast cancer. It was argued that the reason for this is that these products may increase levels of oestrogen in the body. The practice of milking pregnant cows makes it more likely that there will be oestrogen in their milk.

Alcohol

This is not really food at all but it is important to discuss it here. The World Health Organisation and other international groups have argued that regularly drinking even small amounts of alcohol can dramatically increase your risk of breast cancer.

However, just how much is it safe to drink? Unfortunately, it seems that just one drink a day can increase a person's risk by 5 per cent and adding on another 10g increases the risk by 7 to 12 per cent. This relates to all types of alcohol – beer, wine and spirits. Some people think that red wine is a healthy drink because it contains resveratrol, phenols and flavonols which are antioxidants. However, it is still alcohol and we can get resveratrol from black grapes or grape juice. A group of scientists having analysed almost 100 studies concluded that there is no lower limit for alcohol.

There are many reasons why alcohol can affect us badly. In relation to breast cancer, it can increase oestrogen levels in the body and oestrogen drives breast cancer. Another reason is that it reduces levels of folate in the body and folate is needed to create DNA.

A review of 98 studies involving over 75,000 drinkers and over 60,000 non-drinkers concluded that the drinkers had a 22 per cent higher risk of getting breast cancer than the non-drinkers. Each additional 10g of alcohol was associated with a 10 per cent higher risk.

Another study of Californian teachers found that two drinks a day was associated with a higher risk of breast cancer. For post-menopausal women the increased risk was 32 per cent and for pre-menopausal or peri-menopausal (just before menopause) women it was 21 per cent. The researchers concluded that recent alcohol consumption equal to two or more drinks a day was associated with a higher risk of invasive breast cancer.

CHAPTER 23
Breast cancer has a sweet tooth

Cancer thrives on sugar. Cancerous tumours are sugar feeders. They consume sugar at a rate of 10 to 50 times higher than normal tissues according to cancer doctor Keith Block. Most people over a certain age have cancerous cells in their bodies but the body can deal with them before they do any harm. Eating lots of sugar stops the body from doing this and encourages the cancer cells to grow and multiply.

Refined sugar is something we never had until the last century. This may seem like a long time but it is really like a second in terms of our evolution. Before we were able to pull out the sugary part from sugar beet and sugar cane, we ate hardly any sweet foods at all, apart from the natural sweetness in whole fruits and a little honey. However, as it is difficult to gather honey, not much of this would have been available. All in all it amounted to just a fraction of what we eat today, in all sorts of foods. Now we consume many pounds of sugar every year. From having none in former times, the average Briton now eats a massive 140 teaspoons of sugar a week. No wonder rates of diabetes, heart disease and cancer are soaring.

Sugar is a bad food. Actually, you cannot really call it a food at all. It contains no nutrients whatsoever and just gives us empty calories. However, it has a profound effect on the body and contributes to so many different conditions that it is a wonder that it has not been banned. On top of that, it is contained in so many processed foods, such as TV dinners, desserts, breads, cakes, biscuits, boxed cereals and even savoury foods like soups and stews. Why they put sugar into foods like chopped herring I will never know. Actually, I do know. It sells more products.

Sugar is not good for us, full stop. It rots teeth. It can adversely affect all parts of our body. Many people know that sugar is not good for their health but think that having it 'in moderation' is okay. However, what does moderation mean? For me it means almost none. For others it might mean quite a lot. The fact is that we have got so used to sugar being part of our diet that having it seems normal, even desirable. However, remember that eating refined sugar is a very new phenomenon, which only came about in the last century. We were not really meant to eat sugar in that white crystalline form at all.

Not an energy food

You may ask, 'Doesn't sugar give us energy?' Many people do believe just that, and think that the more sugar we eat, the more energy we will have. Nothing could be further from the truth. In order to function well we need two teaspoons of glucose circulating in our bloodstream. That does not need to come from refined sugar. It can come from any carbohydrate food such as fruit, vegetables or whole grains. However, one popular confectionery bar contains 15 teaspoons of sugar! Extra sugar is just turned into fat. It is no wonder that obesity is on the increase.

Do you love sweet things?

If you have a sweet tooth, it is easy to see why. We have been bombarded with sugar-laden goods for so long, we now find it difficult to live without it. We are programmed to like sweet things because way back in the Stone Age we needed to know when fruit was ripe. Normally it is ripe when it becomes sweet. However, in modern times we have processed out the sugar, leaving behind all the other parts of the plant like the vitamins, minerals and fibre. We have then added this simple sugar to flour and milk to make all sorts of confectionary and desserts.

Manufacturers put sugar into most things to make them appealing and to sell more products. As sugar can be addictive, it is not easy to resist these tempting offerings. Fortunately, it is possible to lose a sweet tooth. If we gradually cut down on sweet foods, we will find that they lose their appeal and we will no longer even enjoy them.

Breast cancer and sugar

Like other cancers, breast cancer loves sugar. There are many ways that eating it can affect the growth of this horrible disease. Firstly, it makes our body produce insulin, which was discussed in chapter 5. People suffering from type 1 diabetes do not produce enough insulin and so need injections. Those suffering from type 2 diabetes often have enough insulin but it does not get into the cells. Their cells become resistant to it. Insulin is very important. We need it in order to be able to use sugar and to help it get into our cells. The more sugar we eat, the more insulin we need. This is good as far as it goes but too much insulin is a bad thing.

You might well wonder why something that we really need can be so bad. The fact is that like many things in life, we need a certain amount. Too little is bad but also too much is bad. Nature did not give us sugar in the refined form that we eat it today. The white crystals that we put on the table, which we put in our tea and coffee, which we make cakes and puddings with, and which manufacturers put into just about everything, did not exist in that form for most of our time on this planet. As we said earlier, it is a very new food.

If you eat sugar in this form in tea, coffee, cakes, biscuits, sweets etc, it will make the sugar in our blood rise very high, very quickly. So in order to deal with this sugar and help it get into the cells, your pancreas has to produce more and more insulin – far too much in fact.

Insulin-like growth factor 1 (IGF-1)

We have already said that most breast cancers are oestrogen-positive. This means that oestrogen causes tumours to grow and divide. The problem is that insulin can act like oestrogen in the body and do what oestrogen does – i.e. make breast tumours grow. For women with oestrogen-positive breast cancer this is not good. The more insulin a woman has floating around in her body, the faster cancer cells can grow.

Even worse, another substance we've looked at before is important here. It is called insulin-like growth factor 1, or IGF-1. The body produces this naturally and in normal levels it helps manufacture body tissue. However, at high levels this hormone can cause oestrogen-positive breast cancers to grow. Eating too much sugar and foods that quickly convert to glucose can raise this too high. Dr Christine Horner has said that scientists have found that nothing promotes breast cancer more than this. Women with high levels of this hormone in their blood may respond less well to the drug tamoxifen, given after treatment to reduce oestrogen. A study in *The Lancet Oncology* found that high blood levels of IGF-1 are associated with breast cancer risk but only for oestrogen receptor-positive tumours. Therefore, women need to take steps to reduce sugar, insulin and IGF-1 and the following pages will show you how. If you are diabetic or on medication, I suggest that you discuss any dietary changes with your doctor.

Sugar and weight gain

We all know that sugar makes us fat. It used to be thought that fat caused weight gain. However, since the 1960s, some scientists and nutritionists have been saying that it is not fat but sugar and breads that cause so much obesity in Western societies.

But what has this to do with breast cancer? The answer is that fat in the body acts like an oestrogen factory, especially in women after the menopause, and it seems that the drug letrozole, which is designed to prevent a woman's male hormones converting to oestrogen, may not work as well in overweight women.

Studies have also shown that women who eat more sugar after the menopause also have denser breasts than those who do not. This is not good because it is more difficult to see a tumour on a mammogram in a denser breast.

Is all sugar bad?

Some might think that other forms of sugar such as molasses, honey, fructose and brown sugar are better than ordinary white table sugar (sucrose). They are not. They all do as much damage as each other. Although molasses has quite high levels of some minerals like iron, it is still sugar and will raise your blood sugar too high, too quickly. One of the worst types of sugar of all is high fructose corn syrup. Some scientists believe that this is the cause of much of the health problems in the Western world today. It turns up in all sorts of manufactured foods and it is best to avoid it like the plague.

Some might say, however, that fruit and vegetables contain sugar and, indeed, they do. Anything that tastes sweet has a form of sugar in it. Carrots certainly do. However, the sugar is bound up together with lots of fibre, which means that it takes more time to be digested, and is therefore less likely to shoot right into the bloodstream and raise the blood sugar sky-high. Carrots are also more filling than sweets and so the overall amount of sugar that you are able to ingest is much less. Having said that, some fruit and vegetables, such as white potatoes and bananas, can cause rapid spikes in blood sugar, if eaten alone. It is better to eat them in a meal containing protein, such as fish or chicken.

Giving up sugar

The good news is that it is not difficult to lose a sweet tooth after not eating sugar for a while. If you reduce sugar you start to dislike it and often foods that tasted great before become too sweet and sickly and you begin to feel strange after eating them.

In addition, there are many other health benefits from not eating sugar. You should be much healthier overall, have more energy, suffer less from yeasty problems such as thrush and athlete's foot, bloating and wind and you should reduce your chances of getting type 2 diabetes and heart disease.

Hidden sugar

Cutting out sugar, however, is easier said than done because so much of it is actually hidden. Sugar, sugar, everywhere. It really is. It is hidden in foods such as spaghetti sauce, tomato ketchup (which can contain more sugar than ice cream), breadcrumbs on fish batter, processed cheeses, ham and meat, canned soup, yogurts, salad dressings, most prepared meals, medicines and in fact anything which contains the 'ose' group of chemicals, such as sucrose, maltose, fructose and dextrose. So you can see how easy it is to be eating sugar at every meal without even realising it.

Keep your blood sugar stable

I know that for many, giving up sugar is not easy. We are all in the same boat. We all get tempted by the food industry. Often women who are naturally slim and have never had to diet but like sugar find giving up the most difficult. Others who have always had to watch their weight and have eaten less sugar may find it easier.

One way that can help you to stop craving sweet things (if you do) is to keep your blood sugar very stable throughout the day. It is when our blood sugar drops too low that we start to want something sweet. A craving for sugar can be caused by the fact that your blood sugar has dropped. I am not talking about those who suffer from diabetes here but non-diabetics who just have trouble balancing their blood sugar.

Low blood sugar

Do you feel weak and dizzy if you have not eaten for more than five hours? Do you also get aggressive, weepy and shaky or have cold sweats when you do not eat? If you do, you might have trouble keeping your blood sugar stable. As I previously mentioned, we need to have about two teaspoons of sugar in the form of glucose in our blood at all times to feel well and to function properly. This can come from any food containing carbohydrates. If we don't eat for too long we might start to get symptoms of low blood sugar.

Low blood sugar, sometimes called 'hypoglycaemia', refers to a low level of glucose in the bloodstream. This is not a disease but a very common condition, which can cause many symptoms such as headaches, depression, anxiety and irritability. Other symptoms might be excessive sweating, mental confusion, blurred vision, fatigue, hyperactivity, mood swings and poor memory. You can often see this in children if they need a meal. They cry, get irritable, fight and scream. We have all experienced it.

A rise in insulin

You might wonder why low blood sugar is not good for us when I have just said that too much sugar can cause cancer. Surely too little would be better? The problem is that if our blood sugar drops too low we immediately want to eat anything sugary that is not nailed down. So we grab anything that we can find, and if these are chocolates or biscuits, or even worse boiled sweets, and we eat a lot of them, the sugar shoots straight into our bloodstream very quickly, causing what is called a spike. These spikes in blood sugar cause a rise in insulin which can increase the risk of cancer.

What we really need is for our blood sugar to stay very stable throughout the day. It should drop a little before a meal and then rise a little after a meal. It should not drop very low and then rise sky high after eating. If this happens, we feel as if we are on a roller coaster all day long.

Tips on keeping your blood sugar stable

- It is best to avoid sugar in all its forms as much as possible – white, brown, raw, honey, molasses, maltose, corn syrup, dextrose, sorbitol and especially high fructose corn syrup.

- Try to avoid foods that contain lots of sugar like sweets, biscuits, cakes, soft drinks and tomato ketchup.

- Dilute fruit juices 50:50 with water if you drink them at all. Although they are just fruit, it takes quite a few oranges to make one drink. This concentrates the sugar, leaving behind the fibre.

- Eat wholemeal, dense bread (if at all) and brown rice rather than white flour products – white pasta, cakes, biscuits and noodles – as they turn to glucose very quickly.

- Reduce high sugar fruit and vegetables like white potatoes and bananas and eat them with a meal if you do eat them. On their own they can also make our blood sugar rise too high, too quickly.

- Have regular meals containing protein (fish, free-range chicken, eggs, tofu, soya, nuts) and complex carbohydrates (brown rice, millet, legumes, kidney beans, quinoa and lentils). Some might benefit from eating six small meals throughout the day and nutritious snacks such as seeds and yogurt.

- Eat a good breakfast containing protein and complex carbohydrates as above. Breakfast is important for controlling blood sugar. You have been fasting all night while asleep, so breakfast is literally that – breaking a fast.

- Regular exercise can help stabilise blood sugar, lower insulin and diminish cravings. However, do not do it on an empty stomach.

- Eat avocados, which contain a sugar that depresses insulin production.

- Add cinnamon to meals as this can help keep blood sugar stable.

- I know that it is not easy when we are out and about or travelling on planes or trains. I often get very hungry at this time. A high protein sandwich with one slice of bread will keep your blood sugar more stable than a chocolate bar.

- Consider taking a multivitamin/mineral supplement containing chromium.

CHAPTER 24

Oil is a slippery customer

The topic of fats and oils really concerns me. This is because we are being bombarded with conflicting advice from various different sources. It is worrying that women who really want to eat the right foods are being given false information. There is so much confusion about fats and oils and so much misinformation that it really is quite serious.

The essential oils that nature gave us

As we saw in chapter 13, there are two types of oil which we have to get from our diet. These are omega-3 and omega-6. These are called 'essential fatty acids'. They are called 'essential' became we need them but cannot make them in our bodies. We get omega-3 from oily fish, which contains the important chemicals EPA and DHA. However, the omega-3 in flaxseeds and walnuts does not contain EPA or DHA. These have to be made in the body by conversion from the fatty acid alpha-Linolenic acid (ALA) found in nuts and seeds.

Essential fatty acids		Non-essential fatty acids
Omega-3	Omega-6	Omega-9
Salmon	Most nuts and seeds	Olive oil
Sardines and herring	Hemp seeds	
Anchovies	Flaxseeds	
Mackerel		
Flaxseeds and hemp seeds		

Omega-6, on the other hand, comes from nuts in general and fresh seeds. The particular seeds that give us omega-6 are sunflower, sesame, pumpkin, walnuts, soya beans, wheat germ and corn. These nuts and seeds are found in nature and, in the past, these would have been our only source of omega 6. By this I mean just the seeds themselves and not oils extracted from them.

The ratio of omega-6 to omega-3 in our diet used to be 1:1 which means that we used to consume the same amount of each. Now we consume 20 to 40 times as much omega-6 as omega-3. This means that very many women are overloaded with omega-6 fats and are deficient in omega-3. Many health problems that we suffer from today can be attributed to this dramatic change in our diet.

How did we get our omegas?

Our omega-3s used to be taken care of by eating oily fish and omega-6 by eating nuts and seeds. In the natural situation, before the advent of processing, there would have been no oils in the diet. There would have been nuts and seeds but no oil squeezed out from them because we did not have the technology to do it. This means that there was no sunflower, corn or rapeseed oil, and no foods made from them. Now there are huge bottles of these in every supermarket and masses of foods made from them.

You can see therefore that the difference between what we ate then and what we eat now is huge. Moreover, the nuts and seeds that we did eat would have been fresh and natural, and not roasted, salted or processed in any way. You can probably see now why the ratio of omega-3 to omega-6 is so different. Our ancestors would never have managed to eat enough nuts to make the ratio 20:1 against omega-3.

What changed?

We lived like that for thousands of years. Then around the beginning of the twentieth century, something changed. Firstly, manufacturers became able to squeeze the oil out of nuts and seeds and use it to make different types of food. Fish oil was not used because this would have given food an unpleasant fishy taste. Therefore, they used oils like sunflower, corn and later rapeseed.

We later learned how to extract the oil more quickly using machines and chemical solvents. This changed the oil dramatically. It became as nothing found in nature. Now oil goes through many processes: distilling, degumming, refining, bleaching and, because it smells bad at this point, deodorising. Preservatives are added and then the oil is defoamed. As you can tell, this is quite a lot of processing for a simple little sunflower seed. Even so, oils are used extensively and put into just about every manufactured food in the supermarket.

What happens after that?

The defoaming is not the end of the story. There is more to come. At this point, the oil is still liquid. However, in order to get it to look like butter and spread like butter, it is blasted with hydrogen atoms. Now we have a hydrogenated fat or a trans fat. The history of this is quite interesting.

The Emperor Napoleon III wanted to find a cheap substitute for butter. This was because butter was expensive to produce, requiring cows and land for them to graze on. Therefore, he offered a prize to anyone who could make something similar. Margarine was the result. It might look similar to butter but it is actually very different. Although cheap, it has been controversial right from the beginning. From 1886 until 1948, Canadian law banned all margarines. There was much feuding between the butter industry and the margarine industry for many years.

Today we have the processed oils like sunflower, corn and rapeseed that you can buy for frying and the solid hydrogenated fats for spreading. In addition to these, you have all the foods in the supermarket that contain these oils – a massive amount. This adds up to a huge deluge of omega-6 fats in the modern diet. No wonder we are all so deficient in omega-3, no wonder we are told to take supplements of it for arthritis and no wonder mums are giving extra to their children for brain development. Any omega-3 that we do eat has to compete in the cell membranes with that huge amount of omega-6.

Often you will see on a tub of margarine, 'high in polyunsaturates', to make us think that what we are buying is good, but it isn't. The sad thing is that women who buy them are often the ones who really want to eat healthily. Margarines are often recommended by food writers in magazines and leaflets as a healthy alternative to butter. They are not. These writers do not seem to understand the difference between unsaturated fat from natural unprocessed nuts and seeds and these processed oils.

Rapeseed oil

In the past few years, there has been an explosion in the use of rapeseed oil (previously known as canola oil, which is short for Canada oil as it was first grown there). Sales of rapeseed oil are soaring because people think it is healthy, and magazines and pamphlets often say it is on a par with olive oil. This is not true. Rapeseed oil is made in the same way as all other processed oils. These oils have undergone so many chemical processes that they end up like nothing found in nature. Consuming oil that has been heated to high temperatures and has gone through all the other manufacturing processes is not good.

Foods that contain processed oils

This includes just about everything that is made in a factory. When I taught nutrition, I suggested that an interesting exercise for students would be to go round a supermarket and write down all the foods that contained processed oils. Actually, it might have been easier to look for foods that did not. These oils turn up everywhere. The list below is not complete but it is a good start:

Foods with processed oils			
cakes	biscuits	desserts	ice cream
bread	ready meals	all fried foods	crisps
savoury snacks	chips	pies	quiche
pizza	samosas	fried fish	goujons
fish balls	onion rings	houmous	taramasalata

Foods with processed oils			
chopped liver	dips	soup	some stews
chocolate	sardines in oil	chopped herring	some cereals
non-dairy creamers	salad dressings	mayonnaise	margarine
all oils except olive	sauces	cook-in sauces	pasta sauce

You can see now how difficult it is to avoid these fats and how they can crowd out the fats we should be eating. For thousands of years we ate in a particular way but this has been changed dramatically. This change in our consumption of fats and oils is probably one of the biggest dietary mistakes that we have made throughout history.

Now you have read this list, you will be wondering what there is left to eat and I do not blame you. Only you can decide how much (if any) of the foods you want to have in your body. I would recommend that you keep away from them totally and make your own food. Some of the foods listed can be made easily at home. For example, houmous can be made by blending sesame seeds, organic chickpeas, garlic powder and lemon juice. It takes very little time. Salad dressings could just be olive oil and balsamic vinegar. A small amount of organic butter can be used for spreading. Soups and stews are easy to make at home. You can now buy ready-made pizza dough made with olive oil. You just roll it out and add whatever toppings you like. Ice cream is not easy to make yourself, but anyway I do not recommend it as it is high in sugar.

Saturated fat

This is the kind of fat found in meat, eggs, butter, cream and cheese. Almost everywhere you will be told to 'cut down on saturated fat'. There has been a great deal of controversy about this type of fat and some have argued that too much will cause heart disease, cancer and a host of other ailments. Recent theorists have questioned this, arguing that we have survived on these fats for thousands of years so why would they now be considered unhealthy. They are actually better for us than any processed fats, which we do not need at all. We do need some saturated fat in our diet.

One Japanese study described in the journal *Cancer Science* found that those eating vegetable oil had an increased risk of breast cancer, but those eating saturated fat did not. Saturated fat, however, is very high in calories and will contribute to weight gain if you eat too much of it, but it is still vastly preferable to any processed oils or fats. Another reason for not eating large quantities of saturated fat is that it can promote inflammation.

We do need the right omega-6 fats

It is important to remember that we do need some omega-6 fats, but only in the right form. This is found in the natural nuts and seeds that we have eaten since time began, and not in factory-manufactured oils not found in nature.

To get the right omega-6 fats you need to eat some fresh nuts and seeds. Omega-6 is converted in the body to gamma-linolenic acid (GLA) and this is sometimes recommended to help pre-menstrual tension. Evening primrose oil and borage oil are the richest sources of these fats. However, you usually do not need to buy supplements of these oils. Seeds such as sunflower, sesame (also high in calcium), hemp and nuts will give you your omega-6 oils.

Why are fats and oils so important?

In some ways, fats and oils are even more important than other nutrients because we are made from billions of cells and these cells have a membrane. This membrane is like a guardian. It allows in only what we need and keeps out what we do not need. It is a fatty membrane made from whatever fat is available to it. If we eat the wrong fats, it will be made from those. This could make the membrane function poorly and cause all sorts of problems. Research has shown that low levels of the right fats can cause heart disease, fatigue, ADHD and learning difficulties in children, autoimmune diseases like multiple sclerosis, and cancer. Since our brains contain 60 per cent fat, we should give it the fat it really needs. Sadly, processed oils are now taking the place of the real fats we need, both in the supermarket and in our cells.

What about breast cancer?

With regard to breast cancer, one study carried out at Wenzhou University in China looked at 274,135 women from different countries. They wanted to see whether omega-6 was related to this disease. It was a huge study involving six prospective case-control studies and five cohort studies where women had to write down all they had eaten over a period of time. The results showed that the ratio of omega-3 to omega-6 was important and those with a high omega-3 in relation to omega-6 had a lower risk than those with the opposite.

Another study described in the *Annual Review of Nutrition* looked at many other studies in current scientific literature. After doing a systematic review of epidemiological evidence, it found that those eating trans fats after diagnosis had a 45 per cent increased risk of dying from breast cancer, while 75 per cent had an increased risk of death from all causes. More evidence from the San Francisco Bay area found that breast cancer risk was increased if the women there cooked with hydrogenated fats or vegetable/corn oil.

Finally, a French study as part of the INSERM research agency looked at the diets of 500,000 women in ten countries and found that hydrogenated vegetable oils were associated with double the risk of breast cancer.

What should we do to protect our breasts?

We need to keep away from processed oils as much as possible. It is best not to eat fried foods, margarine, vegetable oil spreads or foods made with them. People often ask me about the best oil for frying fish and chips. I tell them that no proper nutritionist would recommend frying at all. There is no oil that can be heated at high temperatures and do you any good. I do not like to disappoint people but I have your good health at heart (literally). Dr Christine Horner argues that trans fats are the most dangerous of all fats. She quotes an example from the Centre for Science in the Public Interest, USA that banning trans fats would reduce deaths in the USA by 50,000 each year. They are now banned in many European countries like Sweden, Switzerland and Austria, but not in the UK. However, some supermarkets like Marks and Spencer, Waitrose and the Co-op advertise that their products are completely free of them.

CHAPTER 25

Stress

It often makes me smile when articles say that we need to reduce the stress in our lives. They are right, of course, because high levels of stress can cause heart disease, cancer and a host of other ailments. However, we all know that trying to reduce stress is easier said than done. We do not choose to be stressed, we do not choose to have challenges that worry us and cause us anxiety. If we have money problems, difficult children or a demanding job, it is not very easy just to say, 'Now I am going to reduce my stress level'.

However, while it is not easy, it is not impossible. There are many things that we can do, not just to reduce our stress levels, but also to change how we respond to stress in our lives. Often it is not the stress itself that causes the injury but our response to it. Different people respond to things differently. Some manage to shrug things off easily, while others worry about the least little thing. It all depends on your individual personality.

Fight or flight

Imagine that you are living in the Stone Age and you venture out of your cave to go and get some berries for tea. You suddenly see a sabre-toothed tiger coming towards you. Your inbuilt stress response sets in. This is called the 'fight or flight' response as it gives you the physiological tools to either stay and fight or run away. Your blood pressure goes up, your heart starts beating faster, you breathe more deeply, sugar is released into your bloodstream from your liver and muscles, your digestion slows down and your pupils dilate to help you see better. This is all quite logical and useful. You need the extra sugar for energy to do what you have to do, you need your pupils to dilate so that you can see better and so on.

The problem is that today our stressors are not sabre-toothed tigers but mortgages, arguments, redundancies and screaming children. However, what matters is that whatever the stress, the response is just the same. Your heart rate goes up, your blood pressure rises and your pupils dilate. You have the entire physiological response in place to help you run away but often there is nowhere to go. You must have experienced these changes many times, maybe many times a week or a month. If you are late for a very important meeting and you are sitting in a traffic jam, the same thing happens but there is nobody to fight and nowhere to run. You just have to sit there and fume. This is not very good for your health.

Why is reducing stress important?

Research has shown that constant stress can cause all sorts of health problems, including heart disease and cancer. One way that it does this is by reducing levels of natural killer (NK) cells in your body. These are cells which bind to cancer and viral cells and kill them by inserting granules into them. You don't want to lose them if you can help it.

Stress also leads to high levels of sugar being poured into the blood. If this happens when we are sitting in the traffic jam, we have no means of burning it off at that time. Stress raises insulin and insulin fuels breast cancer.

If you can, try to take steps to reduce any major stressors in your life. I know that this is easier said than done but ask yourself if there is anything which is stressing you that can be changed. Can you drop something or do less of it? Do you have friends who constantly annoy and upset you? Why keep them? Are you staying in a job that does the same? Could you change? Is there anything in your life that you could do differently?

If you can change things, do. If not, you should learn some techniques to deal with the stressors that remain. Nutritional and non-nutritional factors can help with this.

Stress and nutrition

When under stress it is vital to eat well and ingest as many nutrients as you can. This is because the processes in your body are speeded up because of the increase in adrenaline, and nutrients are used up more quickly. The nutrients particularly affected are amino acids (part of protein), potassium, magnesium and B vitamins. Stress also causes the body to release cortisol as well as adrenaline. This results in the typical apple-shaped type of body, which has fat around the middle, a type of fat that is not easy to shift.

The problem is that stress affects different people in different ways and different people respond to it differently. With regard to food, some women, often those who are slimmer anyway, lose their appetite and cannot eat when under stress, whilst others are more likely to eat more or turn to comfort foods. These are often wheat-based foods like bread or toast, high sugar snacks or cakes. Neither response is good because not eating robs our body of important nutrients and eating junk food does the same.

A good diet can help our bodies deal with stress because we need the right nutrients to make stress hormones like adrenaline and cortisol, and then to produce the chemicals in the brain which calm us down, help us sleep and keep us happy. For example, the chemical serotonin helps us stay calm and enables us to sleep. This chemical is targeted when doctors give patients the drug Prozac. However, serotonin is made from nutrients, specifically tryptophan and vitamin B6, so if we do not eat enough of these in foods we cannot make enough serotonin. Tryptophan is an amino acid, which is part of protein foods and is very high in turkey. It is no wonder, then, that we tend to fall asleep after Christmas dinner.

Helping stress nutritionally

- Try to keep your blood sugar stable and make sure that you eat a good breakfast (see page 123). Low blood sugar in itself can be a stressor on the body and cause spikes in adrenaline.

- Eat more anti-inflammatory foods (see chapter 3) as high levels of stress can promote inflammation.

- Drink green tea as it contains L-theanine, an amino acid that helps produce alpha waves in the brain. These reduce the production of stress hormones. There is not a huge amount of caffeine in green tea but if you are concerned about this you could try a decaffeinated version.

- Eat foods with magnesium in, such as nuts, seeds and green leafy vegetables. Foods high in magnesium are needed for a calm and tranquil life. Keep nuts fresh or buy them in shells; refrigerate and eat them within a short time.

- Eat foods high in calcium, such as sesame seeds. Vitamin D is needed for calcium absorption.

- Eat good quality protein, such as fish, eggs, organic chicken, whey, quinoa, beans, peas and lentils.

- The herb holy basil seems to be able to reduce cortisol.

These are just some of the many ways that chemicals in food can help our mind as well as our body. However, nutrition is not the whole answer. If we do have stresses that we cannot change, we need to find ways of dealing with them so that they affect us less.

Two of the most important things that will help are taking regular exercise and getting enough sleep. I have dedicated whole chapters to these in chapters 26 and 27 respectively. There are also other techniques which can help.

Emotional Freedom Technique (EFT)

This is a very popular method of relieving stress and anxiety. It involves tapping on acupressure points. Many good books have been written about this and there are demonstrations on the Internet. It is easy to learn and can be very effective.

Meditation

Very many studies have found that Transcendental Meditation (TM) is more effective for helping with stress than any other meditation or stress-reducing technique. According to Dr Christine Horner, TM significantly reduces anxiety, depression and insomnia. It can be expensive to learn, however. If you cannot afford it, there are other ways to meditate which could be quite effective.

One is deep breathing. Breathe through your nose down into the centre of your abdomen. With each breath, imagine that water is flowing down into a clear mountain lake. If your thoughts wander, just bring your mind back to the lake. There are many books and tapes which show you how to do this properly. I would advise everyone to try them.

Listening to music

Music has an effect on our emotions and our levels of stress. A review of 22 different studies found that music alone and music with other relaxation techniques significantly reduced stress arousal. You will know yourself which type of music relaxes you the most and which you prefer but you can be rest assured that when you are listening to music, it's not just giving you pleasure, it's doing you good.

Yoga

New research published in the *Journal of Clinical Oncology* has found that breast cancer survivors who practised hatha yoga were able to reduce their fatigue and lower their inflammation. The good thing about this study was that it was a randomised controlled trial which compared a group of survivors who were practising yoga with a group who were not (the controls). The study found that doing yoga for as little as three months was able to reduce fatigue and lower inflammation quite substantially. On average, inflammation was reduced by 20 per cent. The participants practised in small groups twice a week for 12 weeks.

Another analysis found that those who practised yoga more often had larger changes in fatigue. They also slept better than those in the control group. Of all the different parts of yoga – meditation, breathing, stretching and strengthening, the breathing and meditation parts were believed to be the most important.

Cancer and your emotions

Our minds are not separate from our bodies. Our bodies affect our minds and our minds affect our bodies. If we are not well nourished, we can become depressed, anxious and low. If we worry too much, get annoyed or harbour resentment, this can affect our immune cells. A new field of study has been developed and this is called psychoneuroimmunology, which just means that our mind can affect our immune system.

Our immune system is 'listening in' to all our thoughts, whether positive or negative. This can affect how it functions. Research has shown that negative emotions like anger and resentment can lower levels of natural killer cells. As previously mentioned, these cells are important as they can seek out and destroy cancer and viral cells. As we have seen, the way we respond to stress within reason is often more important than the stress itself.

Having positive and achievable goals is a good way to feel good about yourself. Do things that you have always wanted to do. Give yourself permission to enjoy yourself. Harbouring grudges or resentment hurts us more than anyone else. Your unconscious brain hears what your conscious brain tells it. Give it nice thoughts to feed on.

They say that laughter is the best medicine and in fact research has shown that laughing aloud actually increases natural killer cells in the body. Seek out people who make you laugh, read joke books or watch funny films. Relax, laugh and have fun.

CHAPTER 26
Exercise

Exercise is also excellent for stress because it can lower adrenaline and cortisol, but it is also important for the prevention of cancer and breast cancer in particular, as well as having many other benefits. Whenever I give talks on healthy eating, someone always says, 'You haven't mentioned exercise'. That is because I am mainly a nutritionist and not a sports trainer, but that does not mean that I think exercise is unimportant. I think it is very important. In fact, it is essential for a healthy life.

However, I believe that you should find a form of exercise that you like and enjoy. The old days of 'no pain, no gain' are now seen as being over the top and out of date. As far as I am concerned, exercise should not feel like a punishment. That is why I urge you to find something that you genuinely like.

As humans, we were meant to move every day. Moving helps nutrients to be delivered to our cells and toxins to be excreted. Exercise also reduces inflammation, improves immunity and balances hormones. The Harvard Nurses' Health Study, one of the longest running investigations into lifestyle and health, found that those who exercised for more than three hours a week had a lower risk of getting breast cancer than those who did not.

Evidence

The benefits are also backed up by research. A review of the epidemiological literature on the effect of physical exercise on breast cancer recurrence and mortality looked at six studies. Four of these showed that exercise has a protective effect.

Research has also found that women who exercise regularly for four years after the menopause can rapidly decrease their risk of breast cancer. Even low levels of exercise have been found to be helpful. The researchers looked at information from questionnaires completed by 60,000 women enrolled into a French cancer study over eight years. Those who had exercised regularly for five to nine years previously had a 10 per cent lower rate of cancer. However, if you stop exercising, the problem is that the benefits do not continue. The authors concluded that, ' ...post-menopausal women who do not exercise should consider starting because their risk of breast cancer may decrease rapidly'.

In a large prospective study of women called the Black Women's Health Study, researchers collected information on time spent exercising from 44.000 African-American women over a period of 16 years. They found that those who exercised for seven or more hours each week were 25 per cent less likely to suffer from breast cancer compared to those who exercised for less than one hour a week. Exercise included swimming, running, basketball and brisk walking.

Various studies have shown that women who were active after diagnosis had a 24 to 67 per cent reduction in the risk of total deaths and a 50 to 53 per cent reduction in the risk of breast cancer deaths compared with women who did not exercise.

Exercise helps prevent breast cancer by:

Lowering oestrogen: Exercise is related to levels of oestrogen in the body and about 70 per cent of breast cancers are fuelled by this hormone. In relation to this, a trial from Alberta looked at two groups of sedentary post-menopausal women. One group were asked to do moderate or vigorous exercise whilst the other group did none. They found that the group that did exercise had lower levels of oestradiol in their blood than the group that did not. This is important because oestradiol is the type of oestrogen most likely to fuel breast cancer.

Lowering inflammation: Exercise can also reduce inflammation in the body. We have already looked at the effects of inflammation on breast cancer and seen that this is promoted by the COX-2 enzyme. Fortunately for us, exercise helps lower this, so here again is another important reason to find something which gives you pleasure and is fun to do.

Lowering insulin: Another good thing about exercise is its ability to lower insulin. Physically fit people produce less insulin after eating carbohydrates than those who are unfit. As we have seen in previous chapters, high levels of insulin are associated with breast cancer so doing exercise is very important for breast cancer prevention. Just walking an hour a day has been found to greatly reduce insulin levels.

Reducing weight: Obesity has been associated with breast cancer especially in post-menopausal women. Exercise, of course, can help keep weight down. Overall, exercise seems to give us many protective benefits at the same time.

What type of exercise is best?

Exercise does not need to be difficult or unpleasant. When studies have been carried out on which form of exercise is best, they have found that just moving around in your daily life such as shopping, walking to and from the station etc can add up to quite a lot and counts as good exercise. As far as I am concerned, walking is walking and if you like walking round shops, enjoy it. Even brisk walking for half an hour a day can be beneficial. You do not need to do it all at once. You can go out walking two or three times a day if that is more convenient.

Another great exercise is dancing. Classes have sprung up all over the place. If you love music this is a great way to get active as it does not feel like exercise. With the music and movement combined, some people say that dancing makes them feel like they are walking on air.

Some have argued that the best exercise for boosting immunity may be t'ai chi. Studies have found that this can significantly increase natural killer cells. Exercise which is too strenuous, however, can generate free radicals and deplete the body of antioxidants, so try not to overdo it.

You do not need to join a gym or go to a pool unless you want to. Just put on some comfortable shoes and walk around your neighbourhood. It requires no money, you do not have to get your hair wet and you do not need to drive anywhere. Just put on your walking shoes and go. If you feel embarrassed about being seen walking nowhere, take a bag with you and pretend you are going shopping.

Finally, you will be very pleased to know that even the exercise involved in ordinary housework such as ironing, cleaning and gardening can also reduce your risk of breast cancer, according to the EPIC (European Prospective Investigation into Cancer and Nutrition) study which involved over a quarter of a million women.

CHAPTER 27
Sleep

If you have ever suffered from insomnia, you will know that it is just awful. Not being able to sleep is so debilitating; lying awake in the darkness, tossing and turning, getting up, lying down, trying to count sheep. It is all very frustrating. We have all been there at one time or another. The odd night of bad sleep does not matter if we make up for it the next night but chronic insomnia can be a big problem for many.

According to research, insomnia is so common that it is one of the great plagues of modern living. The 'Great British Sleep Survey' found that more than 51 per cent of us struggle to get a good night's sleep, with women three times more likely to be affected than men. This can cause low energy, mood swings, fatigue and even depression. Lack of sleep not only makes us feel bad but can cause all sorts of physical and psychological problems as well as more serious health conditions like cancer.

Shift workers are particularly prone to sleep problems and they have a greater risk for cancer and die younger than those working normal hours. In fact, the night-time shift is often called the graveyard shift. One study found that this shift was associated with a 60 per cent increased risk for breast cancer. Another study in Finland found that those who slept for nine hours or more a night had a decreased risk of breast cancer compared to those who slept much less.

In another study of women with oestrogen-receptor-positive breast cancer, patients were asked about sleep patterns in the two years before diagnosis. Researchers found that breast cancer was strongly correlated with average hours of sleep per night. Those that slept less had a higher rate of recurrence, although this was limited to post-menopausal women.

How can lack of sleep affect us?

Lack of sleep can affect our health in many ways. For example, it can depress the immune system which means that our natural defences against illness are diminished. As part of our immune system, we produce natural killer cells (NK) which in turn produce substances to kill cancer and viral cells. Lack of sleep slows down this production. In one study, healthy male volunteers were deliberately deprived of sleep for four hours for one night. The next day, the activity of their natural killer cells fell by an amazing 30 per cent. Lack of sleep also raises insulin levels and lowers the repair of wear and tear that should occur when we sleep. However, for the prevention of breast cancer, another chemical that we produce in sleep is very important indeed. This is melatonin.

The importance of melatonin

The research on melatonin is very exciting. Who would have thought that too much light at night could be a factor that affects breast cancer? At night when natural light goes down, our bodies should produce the hormone melatonin. The production of melatonin is completely regulated by light. When it gets dark, our bodies produce it and when it gets light, they stop producing it. Even a small chink can suppress its production. For example, if we put the light on to visit the toilet, our level of melatonin can plummet. Light at night disturbs our natural biological clock and lowers melatonin levels. This is important because melatonin does a crucial job in preventing the proliferation and invasiveness of breast cancer cells. Melatonin is a natural antioxidant and regulates two important hormones, which are related to breast cancer. These are IGF-1, which causes cells to grow rapidly, and oestrogen, which makes cancer cells proliferate.

A study published in the *British Journal of Cancer* found that it can also inhibit the aromatase enzyme, which converts male hormones in women to oestrogen. It also makes receptors on the breast less responsive to oestrogen.

According to Dr Christine Horner, melatonin also makes vitamin D's tumour-fighting abilities 20 to 100 times stronger. She says that it is a 'powerful weapon against breast cancer'.

Therefore, we can see that melatonin does a wonderful job for breast cancer protection. The problem is that because we do not really sleep in the way that nature intended, we produce less melatonin. Instead of going to bed when it gets dark, we stay up with the lights on, the TV on, the computer on and disrupt our natural biological rhythms.

As you know, the natural hours of darkness vary according to the time of year but we should really sleep between these hours. If you can manage it, this would be a valuable thing to do.

Interestingly, female flight attendants appear to have twice the normal risk of breast cancer than the general population. Moving between different time zones can disrupt sleep patterns and may be a contributing factor.

Block out the light

Sleeping in a completely darkened room is also important, so if you have a street light right outside your bedroom, try to block out the light with heavy curtains and/or blackout lining – the darker the room, the better. The silk masks they give you on airlines can also do a great job in cutting out the light. Even with your eyes shut, they will perceive the light, if any is present. I was absolutely amazed and delighted when I read about what Professor Steven Hill from Tulane University said about this.

'Our levels of melatonin are not determined by sleep, as many people think. It is the darkness that is important. During the night, if you sleep in a brightly lit room, your melatonin levels may be inhibited; however if you are in the dark but cannot sleep, your melatonin levels will rise normally'.

So that's good news for anyone who is lying awake for some time at night. It is not the sleeping that affects melatonin production but the darkness. So, as long as the room is dark, at least you are getting your melatonin.

Professor Hill also found that exposure to light at night can make women resistant to the drug tamoxifen.

Some even argue that we should keep our house lights low after dark as bright, artificial lights can also prevent melatonin reaching its highest. Working on the computer late at night is also not a good idea. Strangely enough, the opposite effect happens during the day. You need to get some light or sunlight during the day in order to sleep well at night.

Nutrition for sleep

Improving your diet overall and adopting the nutritional principles in this book should go a long way to helping you sleep well. However, there are additional things that you can do that specifically help with sleep.

We often hear that stimulants like caffeine in coffee and tea can cause insomnia. This is also true of caffeine in cola drinks, coffee-flavoured ice cream and chocolate. Some people, of course, are more sensitive to this than others. Decaffeinated coffee is not perfect, because it contains other stimulants like theobromine and theophylline. However, it is probably not as bad as the caffeinated varieties.

Another cause of waking through the night is low blood sugar. When our blood sugar drops too low, there is a release of stimulating hormones like adrenaline and cortisol and if this happens during the night, it is not easy to get back to sleep. Having a good snack at bedtime can stop this happening. This means something that keeps your blood sugar stable throughout the night. For many, it means having a protein plus complex carbohydrate snack such as a piece of leftover chicken with half a banana. If you wake up hungry, there is no point in trying to get back to sleep without a snack.

Tips for improving your sleep

- Avoid alcohol and tobacco.

- Avoid caffeine-containing substances such as coffee, chocolate and cola drinks. Decaffeinated coffee also contains stimulants. Substitute it with dandelion coffee or Caro Extra. Avoid tea in the evening.

- Avoid bacon, cheese, aubergines, ham, sugar, sausages, spinach, tomatoes and wine close to bedtime. These contain tyramine, which causes the release of noradrenaline, a brain stimulant.

- Eat turkey, bananas, figs, dates, yogurt, tuna, wholegrain crackers or nut butter in the evening. These foods are high in tryptophan, which promotes sleep. Another good snack before bedtime is porridge and a banana.

- Eat starchy foods such as potatoes or brown rice. These can have a soporific effect as they help produce serotonin. Serotonin is then converted in the body to melatonin.

- Exercise regularly in the late afternoon or early evening. Brisk walking is easy and effective.

- Eat foods rich in calcium: yogurt, sesame seeds, tahini (sesame seed paste) and sunflower seeds, but these foods must be balanced with magnesium (see below).

- Ensure adequate levels of magnesium. This is known to be a natural tranquilliser. Foods rich in this are almonds, molasses, Brazil nuts, peanuts, tofu, parsley, fresh peas, bananas, cauliflower, sweetcorn, celery and millet. Eat organic foods.

- Cut down on sugar in all its forms – table sugar, fructose, corn syrup, maltose, etc.

- Drink camomile tea as it has mild sedative properties and can be taken before bed. For adults, drinking camomile tea several times a day is helpful.

- Discuss any food intolerances with a nutritionist as these can make the problem worse.

- Sleep in a completely darkened room. If you do not yet have blackout curtains, the silk masks they give you on planes can help.

- If you go to the toilet at night, use a low-wattage yellow, orange or red light bulb. These bulbs do not shut down the production of melatonin. A salt lamp is a good idea.

- Practise yoga or t'ai chi as these can aid relaxation.

- Take a warm bath with lavender or camomile oils.

- Take multivitamin minerals with good levels of calcium and magnesium with extra calcium/magnesium, if possible.

CHAPTER 28

Foreign oestrogens from the environment

We all live in a toxic world. This is bad because toxins interfere with the normal functioning of our cells. Every year more and more new chemicals are being produced, chemicals which are carcinogenic and which have to be detoxified in our liver. These are in the air, in food, in pesticides, herbicides and other agricultural products. Homes, schools and even hospitals are full of toxic chemicals outgassed from furnishings, carpets, cleaning products and personal care products such as toothpaste, soap, shampoo and cosmetics.

As we've seen before, the hormone oestrogen fuels most breast cancers. The problem is that many manufactured chemicals can act like oestrogen in the body and turn cancer cells on. This is because these hormones work by a lock and key method. In order to give instructions to a cell to proliferate, the hormone locks on to receptors in the breast. It can only lock on if it is a certain shape. It works in a similar way to a key fitting the lock on your door. It has to be a particular shape, otherwise it will not work. However, there are chemicals in the environment that have a similar shape to oestrogen, and which can lock on to oestrogen receptors in the breast and cause cells to divide. These are called xenoestrogens or foreign oestrogens from environmental toxins. It is these that seem to be contributing to the huge rise in breast cancer.

Plastics mimic oestrogen

The author Leslie Kenton tells an amazingly interesting story about this. Dr Ana Soto at Tufts University in the USA was studying breast cancer cells in test tubes. She found that the cells would grow only if oestrogen was present. However, one day she found that the cells were continuing to grow even without oestrogen. Dr Soto soon realised that the manufacturers who made the flasks that contained the cells had changed the material with which they were made. When the plastic became warm, it released minute quantities of a compound called nonlyphenol. Nonlyphenol is an oestrogen-like compound.

The cancer cells had started to grow when she began using these test tubes. She then substituted the new containers for ones made of glass and the breast cancer cells stopped growing. As before, they did not grow unless she added oestrogen. The plastic from the new test tubes was acting like oestrogen. She was stunned by this experience and felt that it was a dramatic breakthrough. Here now was proof that chemicals in plastic could make breast cancer cells grow. This shows how some plastics can act like oestrogen in the body and turn on breast cancer.

These foreign oestrogens are everywhere. We are drowning in a sea of them. So many products contain oestrogen-mimickers including food and drink containers such as plastic bottles, packaging, tubs, pots and cling film. In fact, just about everything that is not sold fresh is sold in plastic, and even fresh items are stuffed into plastic bags to take home.

Oestrogenic products

One study suggested that in certain products some chemicals appeared to be present in very low doses. However, when combined with other oestrogenic compounds, the stimulatory effects were quite high indeed. The study found that there was a higher incidence of breast cancer in the upper outer quadrant of the breast. This is an area where chemical products like deodorants are often used, so they concluded that this might be a reason for it. In fact, some tissue samples removed from cancerous breasts were found to be full of aluminium, which is one of the ingredients in deodorants.

There are so many new chemicals in our environment that it is not clear which ones are safe and which are not. We certainly do not know which combinations are safe or not, so my advice to you is to cut down on the amount that you use as much as possible. We do not need so many personal care products or different bathroom detergents, floor cleaners and polishes. These are sold to us as necessities but how many of them really are? They all stay in the air for a long time after use and can be detrimental to our health. There are alternative natural products that can do the job just as well. In fact, I always found it difficult to clean our white acrylic bath with conventional products until I discovered vinegar. It did a great job and is entirely non-toxic. Lemon juice is another useful cleaning substance.

Personal care products

Cosmetics, hair dyes, skin creams, shaving creams, bubble baths, aftershaves, nail polishes and removers, hair sprays and perfumes also contribute to our toxic load so try to cut down on these or better still cut them out. If you do wear make-up, for instance, you could leave it off when alone in the house. Many of these products have already been found to cause cancer. The International Agency for Research on Cancer has classified the chemical ethylene oxide as being able to cause breast cancer. Other chemicals which act like oestrogen include parabens, phthalates, bisphenol A and aluminium salts. The last one is very interesting because, as we've just said, deodorants contain aluminium.

Our skin does not act as a barrier and can absorb most things from the environment very well. Fragrances are particularly bad for us. The industry uses more than 5,000 different chemicals to make these. Among these are hormone-disrupting chemicals. Skin creams can contain cancer-causing chemicals such as petroleum products that are suspected of being hormone disruptors. It is possible, however, to buy non-toxic varieties of these. Health food shops and the Internet are good places to look.

Here are some products and chemicals to avoid or keep to a minimum:

Sodium lauryl sulfate is a highly toxic detergent used in just about all shampoos, but you can find ones that do not have this. They also contain paraben compounds, which have been known to interfere with hormones.

Sunscreens. These can contain synthetic oestrogens which can be absorbed through the skin and cause breast cancer. On the other hand, you need to be very careful not to burn in the sun. The midday sun is the hottest so it is best to avoid it.

All-over body moisturisers. These cover a large area of your body and stay on your skin for many hours. The chemicals they contain therefore have plenty of time to be absorbed. If your skin is usually very dry, you need to look at chapter 13 and see if you can change this by consuming the right oils. Babies should not be lathered in creams.

Bath foams and bath oil because this involves lying in a sea of potentially toxic chemicals – some of which can stay on the skin.

I suggest that you keep these products to the absolute minimum. There are companies that produce non-toxic products for just about everything, which you can use as alternatives. We are being sold lots of personal care products on the basis that we need them to be really clean and fresh. This is not the case.

Pollution in the home and outside

Studies have shown that some of the most polluted air that we are breathing is found in the home. This is bad because we spend such a large amount of time in the home and of course sleep there at night.

If you have not been well, or have been treated for breast cancer, this is not the time to redecorate your home with new carpets, new furniture, paint, etc. Some new houses after having been furnished give off such a chemical smell that it really hits you when you enter them. They outgas extremely toxic chemicals from all the new furnishings that have been installed. Fresh household paints can outgas toxic chemicals into the house for at least six months.

Cleaning products too can be full of toxic and oestrogenic chemicals so we need to find ones that are more benign. For ovens and other areas which are difficult to clean, you can now buy steam cleaners, which do not need any other products, just steam. Vinegar and lemon juice are very good for cleaning baths and other surfaces. Fortunately, many good books have been written that can tell you how to clean most things without the use of toxic chemicals.

It is also a good idea to buy some houseplants. They clean the air by consuming toxic gases and replacing them with oxygen.

Try not to buy too many foods which are wrapped in plastic. This is not easy, I know. Sometimes in supermarkets, you have to choose organic items wrapped in plastic or non-organic without it. In any case, it is better not to heat food in plastic containers and that includes ready meals.

Other places like nail bars and hairdressers can have such a powerful chemical smell that some people do not feel comfortable sitting in them. One printing firm that I went to had a very powerful smell but the printer who sat in there all day, every day, was not aware of it.

If you like to go swimming, make sure that your pool is sterilised with ozone and not chlorine, as chlorine is a poison which can affect every system in the body. Try also to find safe washing products for your clothes as toxic chemicals can remain on these after being washed.

Cooking

- Use stainless steel pots for cooking rather than aluminium or Teflon-coated ones.

- Microwaves are not good for cooking but if you do use one, don't stand in front of it while it's on.

- Do not fry anything. Fried food contains acrylamides, which can cause cancer.

- Try not to use cling film or buy food with plastic on it.

- Choose organic food as much as possible.

Cars

We all know what a new car smells like. Some people really like this smell as it conjures up images of having a shiny new vehicle which is faster, more comfortable and more modern than the old one. However, these new cars are particularly dangerous. They outgas hormonal disruptors called phthalates which make cancer cells grow. If you do have a new car, leave the windows open and keep it well-ventilated while driving. I prefer to buy a car a year or two old, which is better economically too as cars depreciate most in their first year.

How to reduce your toxic load

You may feel that it is too much of a worry to think about all the chemicals in the home and in the environment but I urge you to do your best. Ask yourself if you really need things like bubble baths, all-over skin moisturisers, hair conditioners, etc. Some women have mountains of personal care products in their bathrooms. How many of these do they really need?

If you want to stay well or get well, you need to reduce your burden of toxic chemicals. It has been estimated that about 80 per cent of our toxic exposure is within our personal control to reduce. The following list is a summary of ways to protect yourself. These are important so bear repeating.

- Consume organic food and drink to avoid pesticides.

- If you buy bottled water, buy it in glass bottles, not plastic. If you need to buy a plastic one occasionally, keep it out of the heat and sun.

- If you eat meat, eat only organic varieties in small quantities. Meat and dairy products are full of hormones, weed killers from the grass the animals ate, antibiotics and other chemicals. People exposed to pesticides such as farmers have high rates of all cancers.

- If you eat eggs, buy organic ones.

- Do not use pesticides in your home or garden and ask your neighbours not to use these. Pesticides on the grass next door to you can affect you too.

- Don't eat peanuts or peanut butter as peanuts can contain the highly toxic aflatoxin. Aflatoxin is apparently one of the most toxic substances on earth.

- Avoid processed meats such as sausages, ham, hot dogs, pastrami and pepperoni. Nitrates in these can be converted in the body to nitrosamines, which cause cancer.

- Choose foods packaged in glass or paper rather than Styrofoam. Why spend money on organic meat only to have to put up with toxins in the packaging that comes with it?

- Air clothes that have been dry-cleaned thoroughly before they are put away.

- Put new goods out in the open air before using, if you can. You can usually smell the chemicals in new goods. I bought a suitcase recently and had to leave it out in the open air for hours to let the fumes outgas before using it. Putting it in the sunshine helped it outgas more quickly.

- Use natural products and detergents. Many companies sell safer soap-based products.

- Keep your home well-ventilated.

- Buy some house plants but do not allow the soil to go mouldy. These clean the air by consuming toxic gases and replacing them with oxygen.

- It is not a good idea to use the contraceptive pill or HRT.

CHAPTER 29
Putting it all together

Now that we have discussed many different foods that appear to have anti-cancer properties, what is the best way of putting it all together? I am often asked how many portions of fruit and vegetables we should eat each day. The government advises five a day but this is not enough. In my opinion, we were meant to live mainly on fruit, vegetables, nuts, seeds, pulses and fish, with maybe a little organic meat. We are now living on foods high in refined carbohydrates, mainly wheat, so that we have wheat in some form for every meal.

As you go through this book, you can see that all of the foods listed are plant foods – fruit, vegetables, nuts and seeds, with the exception of fish. Other foods like pasta, bread, etc take the place of these other foods, fill us up and prevent our access to all the important anti-cancer phytochemicals in fruit and vegetables. Many people tell me that they eat 'lots of vegetables'. What that really means is that they eat some carrots and potatoes with their evening meal. That is not enough. Our diet should consist mainly of foods that pack a punch in terms of cancer prevention. These are the delicious fruit, vegetables and other foods described in this book. We have seen that vegetables are top of the league for protection. Five a day is not enough.

Raw foods

It is also important to eat some of your food raw, as raw foods contain enzymes, which help the foods to be digested. Raw foods contain more of the original nutrients in the food as some of these are destroyed by cooking. Some people, however, find it difficult to digest some raw foods, especially those which are hard and fibrous like carrots. Blending the whole raw food rather than just extracting the juice can help. Fruit anyway should be eaten raw.

All your food should help you

Foods are not simple. They are very complex and act in very powerful ways to help us stay healthy. However, no one food on its own is powerful enough to help us. The recommendation then is to eat as many foods as possible from those discussed in the book. Ideally, everything we eat should help us in some way. However, we're all human and we will want to enjoy other things some of the time. I think that the best way forward is to eat cancer-protective foods as much as you can. If you feel like something sweet, have a squishy prune. A few squares of high-quality dark chocolate melting in your mouth with your green tea could be an after-dinner treat. Chocolate does have some antioxidants from the cocoa but try to find some without vegetable oil.

I hope that you will be able to enjoy your food and look forward to meals as before. Obviously, I do not know what your diet was like before. Some of you might have eaten a similar diet to what is presented here, while others will have lived on very different sorts of foods. If so, it is possible to change. It is not difficult to lose a sweet tooth and after a while a gooey chocolate bar might seem rather sickly to you.

Save your life with soup

I absolutely love soup. Soup tastes great, is filling and warming in the winter, but best of all it can be extremely cancer-protective. This is because soup contains a mixture of different vegetables, all with their anti-cancer properties. We have discussed before the value of synergy. This is where two or three foods eaten together enhance the power of each other. Soup can contain as many cancer-fighting vegetables as you like, such as broccoli, carrots, sweet potatoes, onions, leeks and garlic.

It really is easy and quick to make. Just mix any good vegetables in a pot and simmer very gently in order to preserve the nutrients. There is no need to add fat or fry or sauté the vegetables first. When soft, blend with the type of blender that goes straight into the pot – easy to make and easy to clean, and there you have it. You can add any flavouring you like such as tomato purée, turmeric or any other spice. The addition of spices such as garlic and turmeric add protective power. Don't forget cinnamon, either. Middle Eastern cooks often use this spice in harira or soup. Try it.

I call the soup that I make 'throw-it-in soup' as I just put in whatever I have in the fridge. Once it is blended, it usually tastes nice. If you make a lot, you can freeze it in cartons and take it out as needed.

Your daily meals

Breakfast: Breakfast can be any healthy food that you like. We have become used to thinking of cereals as the normal thing to eat. There is no real reason for this. I admit that it is quick and easy to prepare when we are rushing out but there are other better foods, which are just as easy. It is all a matter of habit.

Try to incorporate some anti-cancer foods into your breakfast (see chapter 23 on balancing blood sugar). Have some protein like eggs, sardines and salmon, with some carbohydrates like oatcakes, porridge, millet, vegetables and banana, depending on how much time you have. Avocados are easy, quick and nutritious. Salad vegetables or cooked tomatoes can be added. Leftover food from the night before is easy if you are in a rush. Even leftover meaty soup is easy, nutritious and filling.

Lunch: Lunches can be difficult if you are not at home. Taking your own would be good but this might not be practical. Try to find foods which are most in keeping with the ideas in the book. For example, if there is nothing available but sandwiches, choose one with lots of good-quality filling including some protein and salad/vegetables, rather than thick bread with hardly any filling. You could always just eat one slice of the bread. Add some green tea.

Lunch at home or evening meals: This is a good time to fill up on cancer-protective foods. Begin with a good vegetable soup. Then you could have fish, meat, chicken, eggs, quinoa or a proper vegetarian meal with mixed lentils, beans and peas for protein. Then choose three vegetables and/or add some salad. Try to include some that are not in the soup. If you have rice or a potato, it should be a small amount to prevent raising insulin too high.

Snacks: These can be any good food, such as fruit (especially berries), nuts and seeds, nuts and raisins or rice cakes with tomatoes or sardines. Keep a bowl of washed raw vegetables in the fridge and snack on these. Really you can snack on anything as long as it is in keeping with the ideas in the book.

Adapting the foods you love

In an ideal world, I would like to recommend that you don't eat things like pasta and bread, but I have to be realistic. Most people do not find it easy to give up their favourite foods for long. However, there are ways that you can adapt the foods you like to make them more protective. Take pizza, for example. In an ideal world, we might never eat another one. But if you really love it, you can buy easy roll-out dough (with no hydrogenated fat), spread it with tomato purée and add lots of vegetables including some cooked broccoli, cauliflower, cabbage, etc.

I am not a fan of pasta as you know, but if you are, why not have a very small amount and add lots of cooked vegetables, pieces of salmon etc. Some restaurants serve huge bowls of pasta with a meagre sauce. Avoid these.

If you like sandwiches, choose one slice of bread, pile it with tinned sardines or other fish and many salad vegetables, and have this with a cup of green tea.

Enjoy it

I cannot stress enough that I hope you will enjoy protecting yourself with these delicious foods. Eating should be enjoyed. It should not feel like a punishment or a chore. I really hope that you will enjoy this way of eating. Trying to prevent cancer, or stop it returning, can be pleasant, fun, but most of all empowering. It puts you in charge. As you look round the supermarket, think of food as something that can help you. Every time you have some blueberries, broccoli or green tea, as well as enjoying it, think about how they are doing you good. Our mind is also a powerful influence. A determination on your part to stay well can go a long way to keeping you that way.

If you have had breast cancer, I hope you will feel empowered to change the terrain or underlying condition of your body. Those who feel they have some control can actually do better than those who feel helpless. The good thing is that it does not need to have complicated recipes, be time-consuming or cause you stress. It can be delicious, easy and enriching.

Finally

We began this book by looking at the general ways to help prevent breast cancer and stop it returning if you have recovered from it. The ways we discussed were:

- Lowering inflammation with nutrients.

- Lowering oxidation with powerful antioxidants.

- Lowering insulin with diet and exercise.

- Dealing with stress.

- Reducing chemical pollution.

- Taking exercise.

- Improving sleep and optimising melatonin.

All of these can have a powerful effect in terms of cancer prevention. The good thing is that they can improve your health in many other ways too. Other conditions such as type 2 diabetes, cardiovascular disease and cataracts can be prevented by eating the right foods.

This diet has side benefits

Often seemingly unrelated conditions clear up on this diet. For example, on more than one occasion, I have seen psoriasis clear up as a side benefit of eating this way. This skin condition is quite difficult to treat medically. You can even start to feel happier on a good diet. Eating the foods we were meant to eat increases vitamins, minerals and essential fatty acids, as well as the antioxidants discussed earlier. This tends to help mood as well as energy, skin and sleep.

This diet helps keep skin soft and eyes bright, joints more flexible and hair less dry. It can also prevent conditions that affect the eyes such as macular degeneration and cataracts (as mentioned earlier). When I last visited an optician, she told me that all the optical magazines were full of information about the value of antioxidants, especially lutein and zeaxanthin. These are found in the yellow pigments of foods like corn and yellow peppers.

You will also be pleased to learn that if you wanted a diet that could slow down the ageing process you probably couldn't do better than this. Ageing is related to oxidation and inflammation so a diet that slows this down can have profound effects.

All of these claims may seem as if this diet is a panacea for every ailment under the sun. However, this is the diet that our ancestors ate for thousands of years. It consists of whole natural foods as similar as possible to the way nature intended and grown in nutrient-rich soil without pesticides. Our bodies still need the nutrients that they needed in the past. Our genes have not changed in this short time. Let your body have what it needs. I wish you all the best of health!

Questions

These are some of the questions that are often asked when I give talks:

Q. Do vegetables have to be raw?

A. It is a good idea to eat some raw as these contain enzymes which help digestion. However, some foods are digested better if cooked. Some people find it difficult to digest very hard and fibrous vegetables like carrots if eaten raw. The best idea is to eat a mixture of raw and cooked foods, and to chew all raw foods very well.

Q. Why do you prefer nuts in shells?

A. The shells are there to keep the oil in the nuts fresh. Rancid oil is not something you want in your body. I do not agree with selling them unshelled. Similarly, if you eat seeds such as flaxseeds, buy them unground and grind them yourself. This is very easy and there are small grinders that can do this very efficiently. Failing that, you can buy them in flash sealed containers without air. Keep them in the fridge.

Q. Which type of oily fish is best?

A. The smaller fish are better because the larger fish like tuna concentrate more pollution in their bodies. Sardines are very good. Farmed fish is not as good as wild as they are often not fed their traditional diet of plankton. This means that the fat in these fish is not the same as the fat in naturally grown fish.

Q. You recommended oily fish. Is smoked salmon okay?

A. Smoked salmon is indeed an oily fish but it is very high in salt and smoking food itself is not good. However, as a special treat occasionally, it is probably okay as long as the rest of your diet is low in salt. If you do eat salty food at any time, try to have some potassium with it. This means some fruit or vegetables, or perhaps some diluted fresh orange juice. However, remember that smoking food in itself is not very good as this increases free radicals.

Q. Why are unhealthy foods allowed to be sold if they are not good for us?

A. There is a difference between food being safe and food being healthy. Legally, food does not have to be healthy but it has to be safe. It cannot make you ill from having gone off, for example, but it can make you fat and cause illness years later.

Q. My parents ate many so-called bad foods but lived to a ripe old age.

A. That can be the case and some people do get away with eating the wrong things. Similarly, some people eat the right things and still get ill. However, if you look at thousands of people, you will find that generally those who eat better, do better. We need to look at trends overall rather than individual cases. What we are talking about here is reducing our risk.

Q. I do not like some of the foods that you say I should eat. Do I have to eat them all?

A. If you do not like a particular food then leave it out. There is no point in trying to force yourself to eat what you hate. I find it difficult to eat flaxseeds so I don't eat them. However, the more you can eat, the better and the more variety of foods that you eat, the better.

Q. Is there any one food that I can eat that will have a large effect?

A. There is no one food that can prevent cancer on its own. The whole diet matters. All the different anti-cancer foods contain different phytochemicals and have different properties, so eat as many as you can and eat some together in soups, smoothies and stews.

Q. You said that butter is better than margarine but what about cholesterol?

A. Butter is a natural food but it is high in calories so eating too much will cause weight gain. However, margarine is a manufactured food, can raise LDL cholesterol and can cause heart disease because it has no function in the body. The cholesterol story is complicated but margarine is not a healthy food.

Q. You have not mentioned tomatoes. I have heard that they are a good anti-cancer food.

A. There is a great deal of evidence that tomatoes can help prevent prostate cancer. This is because they contain an antioxidant called lycopene. However, the evidence with regard to breast cancer is mixed. I wanted to include only the foods that are non-controversial. In addition to this, some people find that tomatoes cause inflammation. They are part of the nightshade family, which also includes peppers, aubergines and potatoes. Those suffering from arthritis are often told to avoid them. I myself do like them and would not make a salad without them.

Q. Do I have to stick to the diet 100 per cent?

A. I think you should do as much as you can. Only you can decide how far you want to go but we cannot know how many unhealthy foods will affect us. I think that the best way is to base your diet mainly on the suggested foods and if you slip up then you will know that most of the time you are doing better than most.

Q. If you had to sum up in a few words the ideal way to eat, what would you say?

A. I would say that we should eat what nature intended us to eat, which means lots of fresh organic vegetables, some fruit, nuts, seeds, good protein such as oily fish, a little grass-fed organic meat and some good organic grains like whole rice, millet and quinoa. This is more than a few words, I know!

Anti-cancer top tips

- Your diet should consist mainly of organic vegetables. Five a day is not enough.
- Cruciferous vegetables are the most important.
- Drink green tea every day.
- Have some turmeric every day with pepper and some fat.
- Eat oily fish regularly.
- Eat a rainbow every day.
- Use mushrooms regularly.
- Eat some raw foods every day.
- Get enough vitamin D.
- Consume a few Brazil nuts every day. Keep them very fresh.
- Try to keep your body fat low.
- Use probiotic foods.
- Do not eat processed fats or foods that contain them. Read labels.
- Do not eat margarine or foods that contain it.
- Do not eat foods with chemical additives.
- Cut out sugar.
- Get some exercise every day.
- Use stress reduction techniques.
- Get enough good sleep in a completely darkened room.
- Cut down as much as possible on chemical pollutants.
- Keep your house well-ventilated and use plants to clean the air.
- Make time for yourself, laugh and have fun. Laughing aloud increases natural killer cells in the body, so relax, laugh and have fun!

References

Chapter 3

Block, K., (2009) *Life Over Cancer*, New York, Bantam Dell.

Maroon, J.C. et al., (2006 Apr) 'Omega-3 fatty acids (fish oil) as an anti-inflammatory: an alternative to nonsteroidal anti-inflammatory drugs for discogenic pain', *Surgical Neurology*, 65(4):326–331.

Chapter 4

Béliveau, R., Gingras D., (2007) *Foods to Fight Cancer*, New York, Dorling Kindersley.

Wang, S. et al., (2013 Dec) 'Antioxidant capacity of food mixtures is not correlated with their antiproliferative activity against MCF-7 breast cancer cells', *Journal of Medicinal Food*, 16(12):1138–1145.

Saintot, M. et al., (2002 Feb) 'Oxidant-antioxidant status in relation to survival among breast cancer patients', *International Journal of Cancer*, 10;97(5):574–579.

Pantavos, A. et al., (2014) 'Total dietary antioxidant capacity, individual antioxidant intake and breast cancer risk: The Rotterdam study', *International Journal of Cancer*, 22;5(5):1823–1839.

Koushan, K. et al., (2013 May) 'The role of lutein in eye-related disease', *Nutrients*, 5(5):1823–1839.

Chapter 5

De Censi, A., (2011) 'Insulin Breast Cancer Connection: Confirmatory Data Set the Stage for Better Care', *Journal of Clinical Oncology*, 29(1):7–10.

Chapter 6

Eliassen, A.H. et al., (2012 Dec) 'Circulating carotenoids and risk of breast cancer: pooled analysis of eight prospective studies', *Journal of the National Cancer Institute*, 19;104(24):1905–1916.

Kobæk-Larsen, M. et al., (2005) 'Inhibitory Effects of Feeding with Carrots or Falcarinol on Development of Azoxymethane-Induced Preneoplastic Lesions in the Rat Colon', *Journal of Agricultural and Food Chemistry*, 53(5):1823–1827.

Monte, L.G. et al., (2014 Mar) 'Lectin of Abelmoschus esculentus (okra) promotes selective antitumor effects in human breast cancer cells', *Biotechnology Letters*, 36(3):461–469.

Chen, D. et al., (2007) 'Inhibition of proteasome activity by the dietary flavonoid apigenin is associated with growth inhibition in cultured breast cancer cells and xenografts', *Breast Cancer Research*, 9(6):R80.

Skibola, C. et al., (2005 May) 'Brown Kelp Modulates Endocrine Hormones in Female Sprague-Dawley Rats and in Human Luteinized Granulosa Cells', *Journal of Nutrition*, 92(5):483–487.

Funahashi, H. et al., (2001 May) 'Seaweed prevents breast cancer?', *Japanese Journal of Cancer Research*, 92(5):483–487.

Chapter 7

Zhang, C. et al., (2009) 'Greater vegetable and fruit intake is associated with a lower risk of breast cancer among Chinese women', *International Journal of Cancer*, 125(1):181–188.

Li, Y. et al., (2010) 'Sulforaphane, a dietary component of broccoli/broccoli sprouts, inhibits breast cancer stem cells', *Clinical Cancer Research*, May 1;16 (9):2580–2590.

Liu, X., Lv K., (2013 June) 'Cruciferous vegetables intake is inversely associated with risk of breast cancer: a meta-analysis', *The Breast*, 22(3):309–313.

Sharifah, S. et al., (2010 Nov) 'In vivo modulation of 4E binding protein 1 (4E-BP1) phosphorylation by watercress: a pilot study', *British Journal of Nutrition*, 104(9):1288–1296.

Chapter 8

Hong, S.A. et al., (2008 Feb) 'A case-control study on the dietary intake of mushrooms and breast cancer risk among Korean women', *International Journal of Cancer*, 122(4):919–923.

Zhang, M. et al., (2009 Mar) 'Dietary intakes of mushrooms and green tea combine to reduce the risk of breast cancer in Chinese women', *International Journal of Cancer*, 15;124(6):1404–1408.

Fullerton, S.A. et al., (2000 Spring) 'Induction of apoptosis in human prostatic cancer cells with beta-glucan (Maitake mushroom polysaccharide)', *Molecular Neurology*, 4(1):7–13.

Chapter 9

Altonsy, M.O. et al., (2012) 'Diallyl disulfide-induced apoptosis in a breast-cancer cell line (MCF-7) may be caused by inhibition of histone deacetylation', *Nutrition and Cancer*, 64(8):1251–1260.

Galeone, C. et al., (2006 Nov) 'Onion and garlic use and human cancer', *The American Journal of Clinical Nutrition*, 84(5):1027–1032.

Chapter 10

Jung-Kook, S. and Jong-Myon, B., (2013 Mar) 'Citrus Fruit Intake and Breast Cancer Risk: A Quantitative Systematic Review', *Journal of Breast Cancer*, 16(1):72–76.

Li, W.Q. et al., (2010 Oct) 'Citrus consumption and cancer incidence: the Ohsaki cohort study', *International Journal of Cancer*, 127(8):1913–1922.

Kim, J. et al., (2013 Feb) 'Limonoids and their anti-proliferative and anti-aromatase properties in human breast cancer cell', *Food & Function*, 4(2):258–265.

Adams, L., et al., (2010 Jan) 'Pomegranate ellagitannin-derived compounds exhibit antiproliferative and antiaromatase activity in breast cancer cells in vitro', *Cancer Prevention Research, (Phila.)*, 3(1):108–113.

Mehta, R. et al., (2004 Aug) 'Breast cancer chemopreventive properties of pomegranate (Punica granatum) fruit extracts in a mouse mammary organ culture', *European Journal of Cancer Prevention*, 13(4):345–348.

Martin, K. et al., (2012) 'Tart cherry juice induces differential dose-dependent effects on apoptosis, but not cellular proliferation in MCF-7 human breast cancer cells', *Journal of Medicinal Food*, 15(11):945–954.

Adams, L. et al., (2011 Oct) 'Whole blueberry powder modulates the growth and metastasis of MDA-MB-231 triple negative breast tumors in nude mice', *Journal of Nutrition*, 141(10):1805–1812.

Azofeifa, G. et al., (2013 June) 'Antioxidant and anti-inflammatory in vitro activities of phenolic compounds from tropical highland blackberry (Rubus adenotrichos)', *Journal of Agricultural and Food Chemistry*, 19;61(24):5798–5804.

Noratto, G. et al., (2014 July) 'Polyphenolics from peach (Prunus persica var. Rich Lady) inhibit tumor growth and metastasis of MDA-MB-435 breast cancer cells in vivo', *Journal of Nutritional Biochemistry*, 25(7):796–800.

Bhui, K. et al., (2010 Nov-Dec) 'Pineapple bromelain induces autophagy, facilitating apoptotic response in mammary carcinoma cells', *BioFactors*, 36(6):474–482.

Reagan-Shaw, S. et al., (2010) 'Antiproliferative effects of apple peel extract against cancer cells', *Nutrition and Cancer*, 62(4):517–524.

Chapter 11

Horner, C. (2007) *Waking the Warrior Goddess*, California, Basic Health Publications.

Barański, M.et al., (2014) 'Higher antioxidant and lower cadmium concentrations and lower incidence of pesticide residues in organically grown crops: a systematic literature review and meta-analyses', *British Journal of Nutrition*, 112(5):794–811.

Chapter 12

Fuhrman, B.J. et al., (2013 Feb) 'Green tea intake is associated with urinary estrogen profiles in Japanese-American women', *Nutrition Journal*, 15(12):25.

Ogunleye, A. et al., (2010 Jan) 'Green tea consumption and breast cancer risk or recurrence: a meta-analysis', *Breast Cancer Research and Treatment*, 119(2):477–484.

Chapter 13

MacLennan, M.B. et al., (2013 Jan) 'Mammary tumor development is directly inhibited by lifelong n-3 polyunsaturated fatty acids', *British Journal of Nutrition*, 24(1):388–395.

Rahman, M.M. et al., (2013 Oct) 'DHA is a more potent inhibitor of breast cancer metastasis to bone and related osteolysis than EPA', *Breast Cancer Research and Treatment*, 141(3):341–352.

Bo Yang, et al., (2014 Feb) 'Ratio of n-3/n-6 PUFAs and risk of breast cancer: a meta-analysis of 274,135 adult females from 11 independent prospective studies', *BMC Cancer*, 14:105.

Kang, K.S., (2010 Apr) 'Docosahexaenoic acid induces apoptosis in MCF-7 cells in vitro and in vivo via reactive oxygen species formation and caspase 8 activation', *PLoS One*, 5(4):e10296.

Zheng, J.S. et al., (2013 June) 'Intake of fish and marine n-3 polyunsaturated fatty acids and risk of breast cancer: meta-analysis of data from 21 independent prospective cohort studies', *BMJ*, 346:f3706.

Murff, H.J., (2011 Mar) 'Dietary polyunsaturated fatty acids and breast cancer risk in Chinese women: a prospective cohort study', *International Journal of Cancer*, 128(6):1434–1441.

Chapter 14

Flower, G. et al., (2013 Sep) 'Flax and Breast Cancer: A Systematic Review', *Integrative Cancer Therapies*, 13(3):181–192.

Lowcock, E.C. et al., (2013 Apr) 'Consumption of flaxseed, a rich source of lignans, is associated with reduced breast cancer risk', *Cancer Causes & Control*, 24(4):813–816.

Wang, L. et al., (2005 Sep) 'The inhibitory effect of flaxseed on the growth and metastasis of estrogen receptor negative human breast cancer xenograftsis attributed to both its lignan and oil components' *International Journal of Cancer*, 20;116(5):793–798.

Hardman, W.E., (2014 Apr) 'Walnuts have potential for cancer prevention and treatment in mice', *Journal of Nutrition*, 144(4):555S–560S.

Thomson, C.D. et al., (2008 Feb) 'Brazil nuts: an effective way to improve selenium status', *The American Journal of Clinical Nutrition*, 87(2):379–384.

Lokman, R. et al., (2007 May) 'Serum selenium level and other risk factors for breast cancer among patients in a Malaysian hospital', *Environmental Health and Preventive Medicine*, 12(3):105–110.

Garcia-Segovia, P. et al., (2006 Feb) 'Olive oil consumption and risk of breast cancer in the Canary Islands: a population-based case-control study', *Public Health Nutrition*, 9(1A):163–167.

Chapter 15

Sulaiman, S. et al., (2014) 'Dietary carbohydrate, fiber and sugar and risk of breast cancer according to menopausal status in Malaysia', *Asian Pacific Journal of Cancer Prevention*, 15(14):5959–5964.

Aune, D. et al., (2012 June) 'Dietary fiber and breast cancer risk: a systematic review and meta-analysis of perspective studies', *Annals of Oncology*, 23(6):1394–1402.

Chapter 16

Koppikar, S. et al., (2010) 'Cinnamon Extract (ACE-c) from the bark of Cinnamomum cassia causes apoptosis in human cervical cancer cell line (SiHa) through loss of mitochondrial membrane potential', *BMC Cancer*, 10:210.

Al-Sharif, I. et al., (2013) 'Eugenol triggers apoptosis in breast cancer cells through E2F1/ surviving down-regulation', *BMC Cancer*, 13:600.

Alshatwi, A.A. et al., (2013) 'Fenugreek induced apoptosis in breast cancer MCF-7 cells mediated independently by fast receptor change', *Asian Pacific Journal of Cancer Prevention*, 14(10):5783–5788.

Bar Graph showing Direct Synergy (p. 177) from FOODS TO FIGHT CANCER by Denis Gingras and Richard Béliveau (Dorling Kindersley 2007) Copyright © Dorling Kindersley, 2007. Copyright (©) Éditions du Trécarré, 2005. Reproduced by permission of Penguin Books Ltd.

Chapter 18

Khalsa, S., (2009) *The Vitamin D Revolution*, California, Hay House.

Mohr, S.B., (2011 Sep) 'Serum 25-hydroxyvitamin D and prevention of breast cancer: polled analysis', *Anticancer Research*, 31(9):2939–2948.

Kim, Y. and Je, Y., (2014 May) 'Vitamin D intake, Blood 25 (OH) D levels, and breast cancer risk or mortality: a meta-analysis', *British Journal of Cancer*, 110 (11):2772–2784.

Chapter 19

Maroof, H. et al., (2012 Dec) 'Lactobacillus acidophilus could modulate the immune response against breast cancer in murine model', *Journal of Clinical Immunology*, 32(6):1353–1359.

Chen, C. et al., (2007 Sep) 'Kefir extracts suppress in vitro proliferation of estrogen-dependent human breast cancer cells but not normal mammary epithelial cells', *Journal of Medicinal Food*, 10(3):416–422.

Licznerska, B.E. et al., (2013 Aug) 'Modulation of CYP19 expression by cabbage juices and their active components: indole-3-carbinol and 3,3'-diindolylmethene in human breast epithelial cell lines', *European Journal of Nutrition*, 52(5):1483–1492.

Campbell-McBride, N., (2007) *Put Your Heart in Your Mouth*, Cambridge, Medinform.

Chapter 21

Dinicola, S. et al., (2014) 'Grape seed extract suppresses MDA-MB231 breast cancer cell migration and invasion', *European Journal of Nutrition*, 53(2):421–431.

Chapter 22

Pouchieu, C. et al., (2014 Oct) 'Prospective association between red and processed meat intakes and breast cancer risk: modulation by an antioxidant supplementation in the SU.VI. MAX randomized controlled trial', *International Journal of Epidemiology*, 43(5):1583–1592.

Shaham, J. et al., (Mar 2004) 'The risk of breast cancer in relation to health habits and occupational exposure', *Cancer Epidemiology, Biomarkers & Prevention*, 13(3):405–411.

Plant, J., (2007) Your Life In Your Hands, London, Virgin.

Horn-Ross, P.L. et al., (2014) 'Patterns of alcohol consumption and breast cancer risk in the California Teachers Study cohort', *Cancer Epidemiology, Biomarkers & Prevention*, 13:405

Chapter 23

Key, T.G. et al., (2010 Jun) 'Insulin-like growth factor 1 (IGF1), IGF binding protein 3 (IGFBP3), and breast cancer risk: pooled individual data analysis of 17 prospective studies', *The Lancet Oncology*, 11(6):530–542.

Chapter 24

Yang, B. et al., (2014) 'Ratio of n-3/n-6 PUFAs @ risk of breast cancer: a meta analysis of 274,135 adult females from 11 independent prospective studies', *BMC Cancer* 14: 105

Makarem, N. et al., (2013) 'Dietary fat in breast cancer survival', *Annual Review of Nutrition*, 33:319–348.

Horner, C., (2007) *Waking the Warrior Goddess*, California, Basic Health Publications.

Chapter 25

Kiecolt-Glaser, JK., (2014 Apr) 'Yoga's impact on inflammation, mood, and fatigue in breast cancer survivors: a randomized controlled trial' *Journal of Clinical Oncology*, 1;32(10):1040–1049.

Bower, J.E. et al., (2014 May) 'Yoga reduces inflammatory signaling in fatigued breast cancer survivors: a randomized controlled trial', *Psychoneuroimmunology*, 43:20–29.

Chapter 26

Peters, T.M. et al., (2009 Jan) 'Physical activity and postmenopausal breast cancer risk in the NIH-AARP Diet and Health Study', *Cancer Epidemiological Biomarkers & Prevention*, 18(1):289–296.

Rosenberg, L. et al., (2014) 'A prospective of physical activity and breast cancer incidence in African-American women', *Cancer Epidemiological Biomarkers & Prevention* 23(11):2522–31.

Friedenreich, C.M. et al., (2010) 'Alberta physical activity and breast cancer prevention trial: sex hormone changes in a year-long exercise intervention among postmenopausal women', *Journal of Clinical Oncology*, 20;28(9):1458–66.

Chapter 27

Dauchy, R.T. et al., (2014) 'Circadian and melatonin disruption by exposure to light at night drives intrinsic resistance to tamoxifen therapy in breast cancer', *Cancer Research*, 1;74(15):4099–110.

Martinez-Campa, C. et al., (2009 Nov) 'Melatonin inhibits aromatase promoter expression by regulating cyclooxygenases expression and activity in breast cancer cells', *British Journal of Cancer*, 101(9):1613–1619.

Hill, S., (2014) 'Exposure to dim light at night may make breast cancers resistant to tamoxifen', *American Association for Cancer Research*.

Horner, C., (2007) *Waking the Warrior Goddess*, California, Basic Health Publications.

Gassman, A.S. et al., (2015 Jan) 'Have female flight attendants an over Risk of breast cancer?', *Gynécologie Obstétrique & Fertilité* 43(1):41–48.

Scott, D. et al., 'Night shift work, light at night and risk of breast cancer', *Journal of the National Cancer Institute*, 93(20):1557–1562.

Chapter 28

Kenton, L., (1998) *Passage To Power*, London, Vermillion.

Index